Julia K. Dinsmore

My Name is
CHILD
OF **GOD**...
NOT "THOSE PEOPLE"

A first-

person

look at

poverty

Augsburg Books
MINNEAPOLIS

make my husband leave - he chose
not to pay child support.
there isn't a job base for
support their families.
ty turns its head, my children pay the price
not "Problem and Case to Be Managed."
pable human being and citizen, not a client
service system can never replace the compassion
n of loving Grandparents, Aunts, Uncles, Fathers,
mmunity - all the bonded people who need to be
t present to bring children forward to their potential.
s not "Lazy, Dependent, Welfare"
aged work of parenting, homemaking and community building

MY NAME IS CHILD OF GOD . . . NOT "THOSE PEOPLE"
A First-Person Look at Poverty

Large-quantity purchases or custom editions of this book are available at a discount from the publisher. For more information, contact the sales department at Augsburg Fortress, Publishers, 1-800-328-4648, or write to: Sales Director, Augsburg Fortress, Publishers, Box 1209, Minneapolis, MN 55440-1209.

Scripture quotations are from the New Revised Standard Version Bible, copyright © 1989 by the Division of Christian Education of the National Council of Churches of Christ in the United States of America. Used with permission.

Page 42: "Let it Be" lyrics by John Lennon and Paul McCartney, © 1970 Northern Songs Ltd. All Rights Administered by Blackwood Music Inc. under license from ATV Music (MACLEN). All Rights Reserved. International Copyright Secured.

Library of Congress Cataloging-in-Publication Data
Dinsmore, Julia K., 1958-
    My name is child of God—not "those people" : a first-person look at poverty / Julia K. Dinsmore.
        p. cm.
    A collection of stories, poems.
    ISBN 978-0-8066-5624-3 (alk. paper)
    I. Title.
    PS3604.I52M9 2007
    811'.6—dc22   2007007991

Cover design by Laurie Ingram; Cover photo © Barb Jucick Photography. Used by permission.
Book design by Michelle L. N. Cook and Christy J. P. Barker

The paper used in this publication meets the minimum requirements of American National Standard for Information Sciences—Permanence of Paper for Printed Library Materials, ANSI Z329.48-1984.

Manufactured in the U.S.A.

11   10   09   08   07   1   2   3   4   5   6   7   8   9   10

More Praise for "My Name Is Child of God"

"Julia Dinsmore movingly describes the hardships, frustrations, and humiliations experienced by the poor. Told in prose, poetry, and song, she articulates with humor and common sense the need for justice and removal of the barriers, hoops, and attitudes encountered by the poor at every turn."
   —*Jane Hanna, former President of the Witherspoon Society and Hunger Action Enabler PC (USA)*

". . . Woven throughout these pages of fascinating stories and first-person anecdotes is the strong and affirming message that God's people bring hope and healing to others, in the name of the healing Christ."
   —*Dr. Richard Bimler, past President and current Senior Staff Associate, Wheat Ridge Ministries*

"Julia Dinsmore's anger, love, pain, and passion for justice ooze out of these gritty pages. . . . Yet, throughout, her generosity and hope shine through."
   —*Andrew Kang Bartlett, Associate for National Hunger Concerns, Presbyterian Hunger Program, PC (USA)*

"This inspiring collection of accessible stories and reflections are sometimes surprisingly touching, sometimes delightfully amusing, but always insightful and spiritually uplifting. You won't be disappointed."
   —*The Reverend Canon Brian J Grieves, Director, Peace and Justice Ministries, The Episcopal Church*

Dedication

To Auntie Sheila Hegna—
storyteller extraordinaire, faithful friend, other mother

To Stan "The Man" Nelson—
adopted uncle, cantankerous Norwegian,
who never turned us away from his door

To John McKnight—
beloved Irish sage, other father,
anointed builder of capacity in community's heart

To Millard Fuller—
faithful servant, liberator of the poor with homes
and vision of love in the mortar joints

To grandparents Bud, Hilda, Marie, and John

To parents Sharon Francis Keating and John Kenneth Dinsmore

To Saint Paul Area Synod ELCA, Bishop Peter Rogness, and
Bishop's Associate Nancy Maeker

To A Minnesota Without Poverty and a brighter future for

My children & grandchildren

Gratitude

This collection of my written words became a possibility because good people extended mad love and support in a variety of expressions. You are appreciated much!

I pray blessings over your names.

Nancy & Rod Maeker and all the Lutherans working to create that new day in our state

The White Envelope Ladies—YES, and AMEN!

Shelly "the Shine-Master" Saunders of cool head, steady hand, and warm, smart heart

Jean & Dede Zamboni—twin guardian angels in the flesh

Pauline Redmond, Betty Stucke, and Sister Rose Tillmans—now ascended to angels in spirit

Ann Braude/Adler who kept a promise

Polly Mann, my first editor back in the day and one of the silver-haired saints of Minneapolis

More holy other mothers—Sisters of St. Joseph of Carondolette, Rita, Brigid, Kate, Jane McDonald, (Uncle Jim McDonald), Marguerette Corcoran & Rita Steinhagen

Sue Whatlov-Phillips, my inspiration

Priestess Amoke Awile Kubat, Minister Sarah "Praise the Lord" Shannon, true Sistahs

Ogitcheda Woman, Sharon Enjedy Mitchel, and broken-down ponies up there in Cass Lake

Ricky, David, Benjamin, and Rale Weiss, where would I be without family?

Sharon Hillberer, who champions folks from this side of the tracks to write words on paper

Meg, Wendy, Bonnie, and Toby—I love you with wild abandonment

Marlise Riffle, Oh Lady, talkin 'bout a lifeline in the desert!!

Speaking of Deserts—Maggie Kazel, Paul Braendstaetter, Julio Almanza, Dr. Joel "Rock People" Carter, Cruz Mendoza, Cher Franzen, Jim & Sally Larson, Rev. Karen Green, Will & Tina, Julie M., Officer Gorden Ramsey, and the Dennisons—Ya'll made D-town livable too!

Sharon Witherspoon, Sharon Witherspoon, Sharon Witherspoon—
Bless your name thrice

Michael Luft, the co-counselor who loved me so well I survived my life!

Baba Bruce Axelrod, The Messianic Buddhist Jew from the Bronx

Linda Bradford, Community Action/Rochester, for saying, "Girrrrl, you need an agent"

Metaphysical genius & prayer warrior, Jean "the Beautiful" Hertler

Markus O'Brian Heffernan, Jan Wulling, Roberta Strong, Annaka Sikkink, Sharaf Pennermon, Martha Fasthorse, Michael Bellenger, Rodney Dixon, Ashley Gilbert, Pat & Kelsey Van Ert, Melissa Borgman, Jamie Wynne, Maryama Green—Props, peace & poetry

Rafalla Green, the full moon rise, the hill, the fire, the story, the lake, and listening medicine.

Dr. Phil Sandro, Janet "the Lucy" Luce, Darolyn Gray, Zenobia Silas Carson, Mary Winston, Mimi Bitzen, Lori Janatopolis—salt of the earth all

Brenda Caya, Amy Ortega, and the Minnesota Parent Leadership Network—You rock!

Trish Staiger and crew from Hastings, for helping.

Pat and Connie, true friends who cater with much love.

*A special thank you to people who read e-mails from Kathryn-Rose58!

Contents

Foreword by Marlise Riffel

WHEN I FIRST MET JULIA DINSMORE, I HAD BEEN TEACHING SOCIOLOGY in the community college system for twelve years. I had begun to see social class as the bedrock of the complex system of oppression that I taught about. Or maybe social class was the busy spider at the center of a vast web, spinning all the strands of oppression together. Looking through my white, upper-middle-class, academic eyes back to my own lower-middle-class origins made me suspicious that class privilege distorts perceptions way more than I had imagined.

So when I saw a nondescript flier announcing Intro to Poor White Trash in the college commons, I decided to go. I remember one of my colleagues, a philosopher, asking me about the title of the presentation. "Can you *say* that?" he wanted to know. I answered that if the presenter, this Julia Dinsmore person, had chosen the title herself, as a way of naming her own experience, then yes. It could represent a reclaiming of a pejorative term. And "poor white trash" was clearly pejorative. That day in the commons, Julia sang, "I'm a Lot Like You," and she was talking to me, it seemed. Now, ten years later, after a decade of learning and sharing friendship, I'm writing a foreword for Julia's book.

"You get what I am about," she told me as she asked me to do this. Yes, I believe I do. But how do I explain what it is that Julia does? She travels unusual paths—moves between worlds even, back and forth between the classrooms of Stanford and the streets of Minneapolis. From dinner at the elegant Scenic Cafe on Lake Superior to the soup line at the Damiano Center downtown. From having a home to being homeless and back again, with three sons in tow. Julia crosses boundaries. Visionary to crazy woman and back, strong and outspoken to desperate and penniless, and back again. When she crosses boundaries, Julia leaves a trail of crumbs to mark a path along the way. And sometimes that path becomes a bridge, a strong bridge over great chasms. Step off the edge of your world and come meet Julia on the bridge between worlds. The proverbial leap of faith.

I remember when Julia, a white woman, was working on getting bus access for poor white kids and kids of color from her Central Hillside neighborhood to school. Kids were walking to school in subzero Duluth temperatures because no school bus served this neighborhood. There was some publicity in the paper and a chance for success. And then she got a letter from a white supremacist group, threatening her and calling her a race traitor. That was a frightening time—traitorous to step between the white world and the world of color? Julia lived between them. Sometimes, because of Julia, I also traveled between worlds. When my best friend died suddenly and left her belongings to me, I packed up the van with boxes of beautiful clothes and shoes and coats, just Julia's size, and we had Christmas that sad and happy January day in her apartment. Those clothes have made the journey between the upper-middle-class world and the world of poverty many times.

Julia wore the clothes when she came to speak and sing in my classes, crossing between the worlds of parenting three sons with no money and no food and no heat to the halls of academia where the heat was on. I saw students touched to the very core by Julia's stories of growing up poor and navigating the world of a welfare mom. And I saw other students bristle as they recognized their own social class privilege and saw them lash out at Julia in defense. Some students begged me to bring her back to class, and others did not want to hear that woman again. You couldn't just hear Julia and *not* react, you see. At a public gathering once, I saw a woman condemn her for attacking the rich. I was used to Julia's keen eye and utterly painful insight, that ability to occupy a place in both worlds and describe the worlds truthfully. But that is dangerous ground to tread. A fragile web to weave. That night it was a perilously narrow, swaying footbridge over the great chasm between worlds. Julia tearfully held on to the bridge. We all did. And it supported our journey.

I've always been amazed, too, at the different worlds of people Julia knows and loves. From politicians and judges and doctors and famous activists to homeless street kids and those society calls insane, and the panhandlers, she makes common ground. From pastors and bishops and priests to those of us who find little use for organized religion, Julia journeys back and forth with her guitar and her stories and her songs. Her friends are a motley crew indeed. We have come to love her poetry and her prose and her music and her e-mail epistles and her rants. And we have all yearned for Julia to be able to speak to a larger audience. To write the book she's dreamed of all these years. And here it is.

What a joy!

—Marlise Riffel
December 2005
Virginia, Minnesota

Quantum Bridges

The challenge to keep one's heart open
In these nazi times.
The heart is a lonely hunter.
You have laid yourself down
As a bridge into
The uncharted terrain of the heartland.
The compass can only be pain,
Your life the quantum bridge
To the places we all need to go,
But simply do not know how.
Your very breath is the ancestor's,
Your tears in public
The steel of the quantum bridges.
Great artist that you are
Your art becomes public domain
Because it is profound, and loved,
And leads over
The quantum bridge,
Which is your very soul.
Your back is covered by holiness
And your steps measured
By the very breath of God.
And in that sacred mystery you walk,
And do your work in the world
Building
The quantum bridges
For the rest of us to cross.

 —Uncle Brucie
  Hilltop Sanctuary
  April 2005

Foreword by Nancy Maeker

DEAR JULIA,

Thank you for inviting me to write a foreword for your book. I am delighted to do so, and I have chosen to write it in the form of an open letter to you.

You are not my first encounter with someone living in poverty. I've lived and worked and had friendships with people of all financial circumstances in Texas, Iowa, Illinois, and Minnesota. What is so significant about our friendship and unique about you, Julia, is that you are the first person who has been able to articulate in story, poetry, song, and truth-telling what poverty has meant for you and your family. You have been my teacher as well as my friend, and I am changed as a result.

I remember the first day we met in person. I had tracked you down by e-mail to ask your permission to print one of your poems in the book I was working on. You were in the midst of moving from Duluth to the Twin Cities, and you said it was a hard move. Little did I know then what you meant by that offhand remark. You also had become disillusioned by well-intentioned but clueless "Christians."

You invited me over for coffee anyway. You told me the story behind your poem "My Name Is Not 'Those People'." You sang for me; you read another poem. Two hours later I left feeling strangely uplifted and energized, though I had heard some heartrending stories. Our friendship was launched.

And it has grown until we have tentatively attempted to articulate our cultural and class differences—like how you always remind us that relationships are more important than timed agendas, or how you like to throw what you call "depth charges" into a perfectly smoothly running discussion, or how we discovered that our assumptions about each other were sometimes based more on stereotype than reality, which leads to the following.

I remember the first time we invited you to give a presentation as a singer and storyteller at one of our Ending Poverty gatherings.

It was to be a paid gig, and you requested to be paid in advance (I think your rent was due). I obliged, processed the check in our office, and gave it to you with the added remark, "Now, you'll remember to show up, right?" No sooner had those words slipped out of my mouth than I realized what I had done. I apologized to you by phone, but it wasn't until months later, over lunch one day, that we actually unpacked my insensitive comment.

You and I had decided that our relationship was solid enough to explore our cultural and class differences. If we could have that conversation and expose the barriers, perhaps others could also—and bridges could be built. So, we decided to have lunch—and talk.

In that conversation I gingerly confessed to you what had prompted my mistrustful remark about the money (because it *was* about the money!). I said that I thought that I—and perhaps others in middle class—fear being taken advantage of. (Yes, that's it; I said it.) Then I told you a story about a man named Melvin—way back in Dallas—who had convinced my husband and me—soft-hearted pastors that we were—to pay him early for painting the church. Then he disappeared with the painting only half finished.

I told you that I regretted to acknowledge that my mistrust of you, Julia, was based on that experience from twenty years ago! Then, instead of being angry with me, you simply listened. Later, as we were leaving the restaurant, you stopped me and said something that still amazes me. You said, "I apologize for what Melvin did."

What? You apologize? No, no, it was I who had confessed. I was the one to apologize, not you! I was the one who had painted you with the twenty-year-old "Melvin brush" and feared that you, too, might take advantage of me—take the money and disappear (and in both cases it was the church's money that I was responsible for). Instead, you silenced my objections by explaining that to seek reconciliation between classes, we need to honor one another's stories, and you wanted to honor mine by apologizing for dear Melvin!

Bless you, Julia.

So, now I want to honor your stories, your songs, and your beautiful poetry. Your work speaks the truth with passion and honesty, humor and humility, courage, authenticity, grace, and love.

You see, Julia, you genuinely love people, and it shows. You love people into changing their assumptions and misconceptions about others, regardless of their economic status. You are a fearless risk taker in support of children, youth, and anyone in need.

You have a passion to end poverty—for everyone—because you see how poverty affects all of us. But you also remind us that ending poverty is too serious a job not to have some fun doing it—so you make us sing—and laugh—and become friends. You tease us about our agendas and schedules, but there is never a doubt that you are pushing, prodding us all to grow—and love—together.

Thank you, dear friend!

Love,
Nancy

P.S. I know that writing this book has been one of the most challenging things you have ever done, not just because the writing is difficult, but because of all of the crises that continue to invade your life and the lives of your loved ones. But, by God's grace, you have done it, and I can hardly wait for people to get to read it and learn from you, as I have.

—Nancy Maeker
January 2007
St. Paul, Minnesota

Preface

The world is what we journey through on our way to love.

HELLO READERS—THOSE I ALREADY KNOW, and you for whom this is the first pleasure of our acquaintance. May these words greet you in good health and spirits, *well to be expected* at this time on the planet! Welcome to my world. Thank you for coming here. Pull up a chair and make yourself comfortable. The pages between the covers of this book contain some of the tellings of my life stories, which I hope will meet with your enjoyment.

Nearing the deadline for the manuscript of *Child of God*, something *curious* occurred. Out of the clear blue, like a favorite old record that's scratched and skipping, my inner ear heard the words and voice of a long-lost friend. *"Guard your heart, Julia,"* was advice Patricia had spoken some ten years previous, during the months my family lived in the southern Minnesota town of Mankato. We'd lost touch with one another since then. After the big waters washed over New Orleans, I'd spent several weeks trying to locate her, as that was the hometown where I figured her relations might still be living. My search was unsuccessful. Nearly a year after Katrina I'm hearing Patricia's wise counsel in Bose stereo baritones and slow motion, which is the usual speed that words come out of her mouth. Slow like how gumbo simmers all day . . . and appropriately spiced. She has the voice of a southern grandma—big, easy, and comforting. I wrapped the sounds of her echoed expressions around me like a blanket and went on with the day.

On the following afternoon my friend Bruce drove from out of town to take me out for lunch. He wanted to make sure I was eating properly between writing and hospital visits to Duluth with my son, who was gravely ill. We went to a Mexican restaurant because that's what I was hungry for. For some unknown reason, when we got inside, I changed my mind and asked if it was all right to go to the buffet eatery located down the road. We did so, and waiting in line to pay at the entrance, I heard someone say, *"Julia, is that you?"* Yep, it was Patricia! The same gold-star-capped front tooth gleamed prominently in her smile, wide enough to bridge time and distance. Our reunion bubbled with much happiness, many questions, and phone number exchanging. I told of hearing her voice speak to me just the day before. Hmmm and very interesting. A thing surely not lost on her spiritually sensitive self. Trisha, as she prefers to be called now, didn't want to keep us from our meal, but Bruce chimed in with *"Don't worry 'bout that. You two hookin' up again looks like a divine appointment to me."* He was used to being in my company when unusual happenings and unexpected blessings dropped in from the heavenlies!

If God himself had advised me what was to come between the time when Patricia spoke the words and now, "Guard your heart" would have been a word for the decade. The world has done its job. It broke my heart thoroughly. It took away everything I ever held precious and did so in a manner similar to the cruelest of joke playing. The world uses whatever we love the most, be it our children, grandchildren, careers, avocations, homes, possessions, faith communities, or health, to do what it does best—bring us to our knees. The world will inflict pain, breed discouragement, cause loss of hope and faith, and it seems to target some more than others for death and destruction. The world is a big bully and a maker of hardened hearts. If it can figure out how to stop us from love, it will. I know that the world worked overtime trying to steal my joy, my praise, my peace . . . and my heart.

So I got beat up pretty badly, but that's only part of the story here. Learning to live *in* this world and not *of* it, is what I hope will shine through my poems, songs, essays, prayers, and little vignettes. This collection of autobiographical shorts is my answer to social unfairness and its result—needless suffering. *My Name Is Child of God . . . Not "Those People"* is my *other cheek* to cruel jokes, hardship, and daunting difficulties. Cheek turning is the act of faith that sourced stanzas of this script, ensuring that the world would not have the last say over matters of my heart. Ultimately, this book is a love song. It is dedicated to humanity's journey through the world. I pray its melody will inspire and enliven our footsteps on the daily pilgrimage to that other shore—our collective divinity.

Many years ago, I decided to value my own life by giving voice to the struggles and triumphs of the daily experiences in America's underclass. The first thing I ever wrote longer than a song was the poem "My Name Is Not 'Those People'." I noticed that the language of creativity was a powerful and effective facilitator for discussing difficult issues such as class, race, privilege, wealth, entitlement, economics, and the beneficiaries of the way we set up our society. My songs and poetry sharing were soon accompanied by true-life storytelling when invited to colleges, faith communities, and public/private poverty reduction initiatives. While learning to tell performance art stories twenty years ago, something stood out that is important enough to mention here, because it is still true. It speaks to the level of social isolation we Americans are experiencing.

The repeated comments from my speaking engagements have been:

- *I learned more about poverty in one afternoon with you than from four years of studying in college.*
- *Why is this the first time I have ever heard someone like you tell about experiences in the underbelly of America?*
- *Why is there so much information about poor people but so little of it in their own words?*
- *How did you learn to talk the way you do, and by what books were you educated?*
- *When are you going to write your stories so they can be used for required reading in college courses?*

God bless the Lutherans for their courage to publish this Irish Catholic member of the white trash tribe of Minnesota (who is known more for using colorful language than for her skills in literacy). Here is my first book! It contains emotional honesty and my best thinking on that about which I feel passionately: rearranging our resources so that every child is afforded the same birthright—an opportunity to thrive!

I hope my storytelling will inspire other poor people to claim and use their own voices, because they are needed and valuable. I would so enjoy their company. Coming out of the class closet, in person and out loud, has been a lonely wilderness experience. If that which conspires to silence poor people had hands, shame would be its thumbs. Shame gave strength to chokeholds that have stilled the sound of many precious wisdoms, and shame detours humanity's progress toward liberating ourselves from the deadly consequences of selfishness. The brilliance, poetry, singing, lamentations, prayers, and praises in voices of the poor go far beyond victim-speak. It is my hunch that our unspoken conversations are blessings deferred and that they provide the missing pieces of a road map that takes us to a home worthy of our hearts!

Despite giving up poverty for Lent every year, its grip on me and mine has continued. Poverty has long arms that reach through generations of people, leaving telltale bruise marks on its victims even after they are blessed enough to get out. Poverty is a powerful teacher when you survive it with your humanity intact. People in poverty are good. It's just that we got a bad rap from the world and we're hurt. It is the deepest hope of my heart that this little book will shed some light into the confusing mix of conversation about who gets to have their basic needs met, who does not, and why.

—Julia K. Dinsmore
January 2007
Brooklyn Center, Minnesota

My Name Is Not "Those People"

For Denise Mayotte, Polly Mann, and parents on the planet who are raising children without adequate social or economic support.

My name is not "Those People."
I am a loving woman, a mother in pain,
Giving birth to the future, where my babies
Have the same chance to thrive as anyone.

My name is not "Inadequate."
I did not make my husband leave us—
He chose to, and chooses not to pay child support.
Truth is though; there isn't a job base
For all fathers to support their families.
While society turns its head, my children pay the price.

My name is not "Problem and Case to Be Managed."
I'm a capable human being and citizen, not just a client.
The social service system can never replace
    the compassion and concern of loving grandparents, aunts,
    uncles, fathers, cousins, community—
    all the bonded people who need to be
But are not present to bring little ones forward to their potential.

My name is not "Lazy, Dependent Welfare Mother."
If the unwaged work of parenting,
    homemaking, and community building were factored
    into the gross domestic product,
My work would have untold value. And why is it that mothers whose
Husbands support them to stay home and raise children
Are glorified? And why don't they get called lazy or dependent?

My name is not "Ignorant, Dumb, or Uneducated."
I got my PhDo from the university of life, school of hard everything.
I live with an income of $621 with $169 in food stamps for three kids.
Rent is $585. . . . That leaves $36 dollars a month to live on.
    I am such a genius at surviving,
    I could balance the state budget in an hour.
Never mind that there's a lack of living-wage jobs.
Never mind that it's impossible to be the sole emotional, social,
    spiritual, and economic support for a family.
Never mind that parents are losing their children
    to gangs, drugs, stealing, prostitution, the poverty industry,
    social workers, kidnapping, the streets, the predator.
Forget about putting more money into our schools . . .
    just build more prisons!

My name is not "Lay Down and Die Quietly."
My love is powerful, and the urge to keep my children alive will never
stop.
All children need homes and people who love them.
All children need safety
And the chance to be the people they were born to be.

The wind will stop before I allow my sons to become a statistic.
Before you give in to the urge to blame me,
    the blame that lets us go blind and unknowing
    into the isolation that disconnects
    your humanity from mine,
Take another look. Don't go away.
For I am not the problem, but the solution.
And . . . my name is not "Those People."

Story of a Poem

"THOSE PEOPLE DON'T NEED HOMES. . . . We give them turkeys at Christmas and Thanksgiving," said the chair of the church finance committee in the early '90s.

I didn't get the logic of such a statement. Like you can live in a turkey? The little ragtag group of welfare recipients called the Mother's Union had just made a proposal to the finance committee of a large, very socially just, and well-heeled faith community in Minneapolis. Asking them to be the fiscal agent for the $65K we'd raised would surely meet with a yes, or so we thought, to purchase a home that might stabilize the lives of a large single-parent-headed family. Bona fide housing experts came along to validate the workability of our initiative. After eighteen months of trying to build principled partnerships with people who had access to money and social resources, we'd learned a few things. Always bring *experts*. They'll be believed, even though we moms would have said the very same things about the housing crisis and about how affordable homes affect childhood. It's called social ventriloquism. Sadly, our professional mouthpieces did not sway committee members.

Someone in our group quipped, "What's up with this? Didn't the leader of your religion tell people to help the poor?"

I responded. "Yes, that is precisely what Jesus told us. The only problem with Christianity is that we're still trying to figure out how it's practiced."

I went home and wrote "My Name Is Not 'Those People'."
This poem was adversity's love child.
Born female.

To my great surprise, this poem eventually became the object of regard to a wide variety of readers, in locations spanning the planet. The long and short of the story is that "Those People," precocious child that she was, is a poem that got a life of her own. After leaving home, poem backpacked around continents. She was translated into several languages, even newly written ones like Hmong. Something of great interest is that indigenous peoples have thanked me for writing verses that speak into a common circumstance.

Hmmmm. So that means poor folk get done the same ways all over the world.

"Those People" got published too many times to count. Her text became the object of studies in temples of head and of religions.

"Those People" became a wall hanging. She was loved much in Minnesota, California, and New Orleans.

"Those People" got kissed into glory by the lips of Senator Paul Wellstone, when she was read into the *Congressional Record* on the floor of the United States Senate one year.

That was one of her shining moments for sure. I didn't even know about the existence of such things until a gold-embossed copy of the *Congressional Record* arrived in the mail one day. Baby girl was growing up. She looked so beautiful in her regal evening gown worn at the U.S. Senate.

After time, "Those People" started hobnobbing with jet-setting think tanks, academic all-stars, and good government. I was a proud parent. Poem got so busy I couldn't keep track of all the places that she went from year to year. It brought a measure of excitement to see her get all dressed up and travel around in first-class accommodations to destinations I had never imagined before. My daughter was becoming famous. I must admit to thoughts entertained about her fame, as I wondered if she'd buy me a new house, or a car, when the money started rolling in. It never did. "Those People" became famous, but I remained as broke as the day she left home. So much for fairy tales and pipe dreams. It's really quite all right how things are working out. I won't complain . . . too much.

I'M STILL VERY MUCH A PROUD MOTHER TO MY POEM. She's lived such an interesting life. I love her so. She's beautiful, smart, and courageous.

Her energy and spunk are contagious.
Caused backbones to stand taller
than they were before they met her.
Uncurled people's posture from positions unnatural,
incongruent with Child of God we all are.
Those People has been around the block a time or two.
Been wined and dined and adorned in fine clothes.
Yes. But to me poem looks most beautiful
When she shines in dignity reclaimed.

AMONG THE EXPERIENCES OF BEING THE AUTHOR of "My Name Is Not 'Those People'," there are two I wish to mention in this section of my thoughts. The first one became the subject of my dismay during a particularly difficult period of my life. Tragedy and troubles had reduced to pulp every hope and dream that is sacred ground of a mother's heart. Vacuous strands of my desire laid down here and there. A ten-year hurricane blew my life and family to smithereens and kingdom come. It had been an unrelenting beat down, stuff that could transform the saint's highway into a funeral procession. In the tailwinds of the terrible storm, I struggled to keep a toehold on the last bit of terra firma beneath my feet, my home. What's worse is that the red clay of my soul's strength, integrity, began to crumble. Desperation's reign soaked my strength into the mush that was the repercussion of calamity.

So, there I was, at the lowest low point of my entire life, when I went onto the Internet and discovered that my poem had been published in a sociology textbook without my permission. Topping off the insult I felt upon learning of poem's latest travels, the biographical information written about the author included information that was new to me. Apparently I had been married and divorced. Oh my. I knew my memory wasn't what it used to be, but I'm quite sure I would have remembered experiencing my own wedding. In addition to reporting my marital status, more inaccurate statements went on to the invention of describing the what, when, who, where, and how of why I wrote my poem. This pissed me off to no end. I became enraged and felt mortally offended. I railed at God and anyone who would listen. I railed at the walls that were all too soon going to enjoy a new owner. After these fits of hysteria settled down, I threw myself a pity party.

And so it went. I survived. I threw my hands into the air and acquiesced will to the winds. I gave up the struggle that was mine in that particular time. I survived.

Surrendering all wasn't as bad as I had imagined. And so it went some more.

AFTER A TIME, I WENT ONTO THE INTERNET to see what "Those People" had been up to lately. Love child that she was, poem had been busy training in some tens of thousands of volunteers in Appalachia and other places as well. She was the name of several conferences and the subject of editorial commentary in newspapers around the country. That's nice. It did warm my heart to know that some things good were occurring, in spite of how terrible it still felt. After the hurricane laid its waste, that is.

Recovery is a slow process. Letting go and letting God,
When there is nothing else that can be done,
Seemed to be the way through pain still fresh in the aftermath of life's storms.
And so letting go is what I did some more.
And so it went. Letting go and letting God.

AFTER ANOTHER TIME, I WENT ONTO THE INTERNET and found "Those People" in a sermon from the mountains of the Ozark. The writer's name, if my memory serves me correctly, was Reverend Hockensmith. I was just fine before beginning the little adventure that was reading this interpretation of poem, but by the end, I was too through. His elaborations on daughter's text really messed me up, and a puddle of boo-hooing I became. This is the first part of the second point, in which I wish to tell about the experience it has been as the author of the poem known on the streets by name, "Not Those People."

You see,
> *The message in the sermon spoke of compassion,*
>> *Second chances, and consideration for the least of these,*
>>> *Which was me.*
>>> *I cried. No, I wept.*
>>>> *From endless depths*
>>>>> *This weeping did endure for a time.*
> *The reverend's words on the Internet that day said,*
>> *"Not those people . . . but still God's children . . . "*
Absolution of my own self-contempt became forgiveness. Rebirth.
I wept some more.
> *Reborn and born again in little bits and pieces,*
>> *I'm becoming restored.*

I have noticed that restoration is a process with its own speed. It is best not to rush the journey to our return. Renewal meanders this way and that. Unfolding trust in baby step ways. I am in the palm of restoration's hand just now. It is a time of rebuilding. What?

I don't know, and I don't want to know. Attachment is the womb of pain, so no thank you.

The design of my rebuilding is Creator's hand to draw.

Terrors incurred from the storm of my century do begin to fade some. And so it goes.

After a time that is most recently, I went on the Internet to read my e-mail. Someone by the name of Reverend Nancy Maeker sent a note of inquiry regarding the use of "Those People" in a book. She and a Bishop Rogness were working on a project to end poverty in our state. That's great. She went on to say they were from the synod of St. Paul, ELCA. Not knowing what a synod or an ELCA was, for some vague reason I thought she was referring to a mountain. *Hmmm, so there's a Mt. Synod in St. Paul?* was my thought. The first responses to her e-mail played out within my head, which I decided might be better left unsaid. They must be nuts to think that poverty can be ended, and what's more they have a date. 2020 is their timeline. They're delusional. The air must be quite thin up there on Mt. Synod in St. Paul. Still tender from the hurt of poem's kidnapping,

I must admit to entertaining thoughts unfriendly. The wound that was published without permission, "Those People" profits pocketing impugned, fruit of my womb's suffering pimped out while I can't even afford to fix the car. Well, let's just say, Rev. Maeker's request hit a raw nerve. I was not yet the happy camper I am almost now. At any rate, but more specifically the rate of this story's unfolding, a miracle did begin.

Conversation conceived in question asked.
   She wanted to know. Bless her request.
      What was stuff that birthed your poem?
The answer being nature of things most personal, I did say,
Is conversation better suited over coffee than in e-mail
   or the phone.
      "Those People" had been born out of wedlock.
        Adversity's love child she was.
She is a product conceived by worlds. Worlds that hurt.
      Stuff of her once upon a time. Worlds
          women and children. Without
              homes.

AND SO IT GOES. AND SO IT WENT THAT I WAS TO LEARN what ELCA is, and that I had confused the St. Paul Area Synod with Mount Sinai. Oy vey. I think this mix-up had something to do with the energy of a certain sermon. Spoken word, from ranges approximating high upon mountaintops. Above principalities power to publish gloom and doom. All was well with my soul.

AND SO IT WENT. I FELL IN WITH THE LUTHERANS, and their meetings, and their crazy idea to end poverty in our state. Which leads me to the point I wish to make about the experience it has been to be the author of this poem, which will end this section of my thoughts. All things considered, and from points of view where eagles fly,

I can see now with more clarity,
    Desperation ushered terribly destructive,
        By storms fierce-blowing winds
            Brought me to this place.
            Brought me safe thus far.
And so it goes. And so by grace go I
    Into this place that is the blessing after the storm.
In time, restoration comes,
    And Murial Simmons said my book would get done
        In God's time. Not mine.
    She told me to relax and wait upon the Lord. I'm learning.
to rest while my sanity gets restored.
And speaking of mental health, I've decided.
To entertain the possibility of approximating
    Poverty's end in Minnesota.

We're working as a family, my daughter and me. And that's the story of how *My Name Is Child of God . . . Not "Those People"* came to be. This book.

Part A. Head Winds—The Promise of a Sure Foot

Spring

Sunshine and flowers and trees in full bloom,
March winds, May showers, and soon it is June.
Gone are the dark days that sick and depress.
Come now the sun with its loving caress . . . Oh . . . Oh

Come alive, become awake again, and be whole—
I hear God telling me—
Come Alive, become awake again, and be whole.

With each new day I'm renewed and remade,
Reaping earth's bounty she graciously gave,
Evolving and spinning with each season's turn,
Fumbling to understand all that I've learned . . . Oh . . . Oh

Come alive, become awake again, and be whole—
I hear God telling me—
Come Alive, become awake again, and be whole.

Coming Up Years

We love because [God] first loved us. —*1 John 4:19*

Queen of the Gypsies

Once upon a time my Auntie Sheila told me how a neighbor had characterized her sister (my mother) just before she'd met my father and had me. Grandpa Keating and his friend were sitting on the front porch of the three-bedroom South Minneapolis home of his twelve offspring, drinking after-work beers. *"Bud, that daughter of yours could suck the oxygen out of North Dakota,"* was his observation. Mother's drill-sergeant orders for date preparations had been shrill enough to wake the dead. Someone had inserted the plastic stays in her crinolines incorrectly, which caused her poodle skirt to hang the wrong way. The sparkly leash and jeweled doggie eye had to be visible according to decree of big sister, and tragically were not. Despite bluing, starching, and hang drying said undergarments the day before, one of the younger sibling servants neglected to iron the poodle to her satisfaction. All Armageddon was released in the person and voice of my mother.

There was no rational reason for such hysterics. Her boyfriend, Tom Domka, had already been trained to wait at least an hour whenever he came to call for a date. Perhaps Mother's charming way with siblings and dates was an early sign of her schizophrenia or bipolar disorder. Auntie told me, *"Your mother would just launch into stratospheric tantrums when something was not to her liking, and you never knew what that something would be."* I was greatly relieved to find out that others besides myself had walked on eggshells around her, because that let me off the hook for being the cause of such curious and frequent launchings. I only wish I had figured it out before the age of forty-six!

Sometimes things we hear in childhood can stay with us for a lifetime, growing inside our imaginations to proportions eventually resembling mythological. My little, literal self formed many powerful ideas this way. Two of these things heard stand out in the recollections of my early years, as they eventually became intertwined with the stories of my life. Mother was their original author. I suppose her words took up such a vibrant life in mini-me because her accounts were voiced during times of stress and were usually illustrated by the sound of china shattering against the wall.

"God Almighty, you know they did this to me!" she'd scream at the ceiling. *"Those Gypsies put a curse on me! It's their fault my life is miserable and I suffer so. I'm doomed. They put a curse on me, all because I would not give up my faith. I am cuuuuuuursed!"* The sight and sound of household objects hurled through the air would give way to loud sobbing and other guttural moaning that was the sound of her torment. We kids took cover behind the nearest piece of sturdy furniture or scurried upstairs and out of sight at the start of one of these eruptions. On occasions when the baby was trapped in his high chair, I too would be held hostage for mother's dramatic enactment of *Curse of the Gypsies.* We were an audience of three—little brother, the ceiling, and me. I would stay for the second act (which did not call for flying projectiles) long enough to make my way over to baby boy, unstrap his wide-eyed self, and carry him to safety. For the longest time I had the utmost of respect for ceilings, because I thought that was where God lived.

Part 2 in the legend of the tortured soul of my mother was a script that told of her surviving *the curse* and other terrible things to come in her life. She would speak of *God's Chosen People* in hallowed tones and reverence reserved only for the holiest of matters and people—like Jesus, Mary, the pope, and the parish priest. She said things like, *"If the Jews could suffer through centuries of horrors and persecution, I can survive my tribulations."* Mother credited them for her survival of desperate times in the state hospital—before, during, and after shock treatments and long separations from us children. She told me, *"When I wanted to give up and could bear no more pain, I thought about the Jewish mothers with babes in arm being sent to concentration camps, gas chambers, and fiery furnaces."* Over the years she shared different versions of the suffering history of the Jews and how thinking on their plights had helped her to endure her own misery, hardship, and difficulty.

I was very young when I first heard about these amazing people and their magical powers. Mortals who could cast curses and reach out from furnace graves and pages of the Old Testament to affect Mother so profoundly got my attention in a big way! These *things heard* became the true-life fairy tales Grimm of my childhood . . . and beyond.

I was the firstborn child to my parents John Kenneth and Sharon Francis. The rest were born in stair-step precision every nine months with a double blessing in mother's fourth pregnancy. I spent a lot of time behind a big brown chair in the corner of our living room— with scissors, color crayons, and paper—when I wasn't folding cloth diapers or setting the table for meals. Televisions and radios in our home didn't seem to work correctly, especially when Mother came near them. The screens went fuzzy and their sounds turned to static, so we learned to entertain ourselves in nonelectronic activity. At the age for my first school experience we were children six to parents who really had no business procreating!

A scar across my left eyebrow attests to that sentiment, confirming the whispered worries of those who thought my mother should never be left alone with her children, especially when pregnant. I was a precocious child in many ways and could carry a tune early, so mother probably thought I could pick up potty training at the wee age of eighteen months. I wet the bed one night, and she became unhinged. She and Father had come home from an evening on the town. The story is that I was yanked out of my sleep and marched into the bathroom to the sounds of mother's histrionics. *Something happened* while my wet footie pajamas were being removed. Auntie Sheila was the live-in baby sitter that summer. According to her, my blood was spattered all over the bathroom she, me, my father, and baby sister Jeanne Marie were locked into by way of protection from further harm by Armageddon launching. I got my head stitched up at the ER that night. It was not the last time we were to be locked behind bathroom doors during one of mother's furies.

My schooling began at the age of four. I lasted all of three weeks in kindergarten. Mother told me about having to barricade all my siblings in a room so she could run around the neighborhood looking for me—repeatedly. I remember wanting nothing to do with school. I was bored and preferred to watch what people were doing out in the big world between the brown chair in the living room and wherever it was my little footsteps would take me, preferably as far as possible in the opposite direction from school. After one too many phone calls from the principal, my community excursions ended.

Mother pulled me out, and the next year I was put directly into first grade at Incarnation Catholic School in South Minneapolis.

Between threats of being sentenced to kiddie jail for truants, and waching the fascinating lifestyle of the nuns at my new school, I almost received a certificate of perfect attendance. Sister Pancracious was my homeroom teacher. She wore the flowing regalia of old school nun-wear called a *habit,* which I thought a strange name for the wedding dress and veil that concealed every hair on her head. Mother had told me that Sister P., and all the other nuns, were married to Jesus. That fascinating statement was my introduction to the concept of polygamy. Sister P. told my parents that I spent most of the school day looking at her from my desk. She felt I was studying her instead of my lessons. She was right. I was waiting for Jesus to show up and didn't want to miss a chance to see him in person! The Son of God's presence had been a big mystery to me, other than the portrait he'd posed for, which hung in the front vestibule at home. If all these women were married to him, he would surely make an appearance sooner or later! The other reason my attendance record improved was that school became a solace from an increasingly bizarre and violent home life.

One morning while my French braids were being put in, my mother and father got into a knockdown, drag-out doozie of a fracas. Father stepped over Mom who was passed out cold, and just walked out the door to work. I thought she was dead. The orange hairbrush with black bristles lay near her hand. I was glad when she woke up. Staying home to care for the younger siblings would interfere with my Jesus-sighting plans. When mother finished my French braids, I was out the door, enjoying the six-block walk to school. On the way, I bumped into several kids new to the neighborhood. *"Are you Catholic or public?"* curious Julia wanted to know. At that age my religion was something akin to a national identity, as I thought there were only these two kinds of people left in the world after all the Jews had been killed by Mr. Hitler. Race and class distinctions were not yet fully rooted in my social being. It wasn't until adulthood that I realized that my two best friends in grade school had been the only black and Indian students enrolled there.

To my child's way of putting into order the world as I understood it, the Gypsies were, of course, public, and the big *other* in my early life. Much of my mother's curse story remained a mystery until I commenced to write this book. After forty and some years, I asked mother to tell me about the curse of the gypsies. We were in the overfull ER waiting room at Abbot Northwestern Hospital. If she had not been in a wheelchair, there mightn't have been a place for her to sit. Looking like we were in for an all-night wait had us both grumpy. Mother does not like to wait for anything, including doctor appointments, so she frequents emergency rooms. Her plan for getting speedy service had backfired, so I decided to try and make the most out of our time together. A good story might keep us both awake. Here is what she told me.

The Curse of the Gypsies begins at the Diamond Jubilee, seventy-five-year celebration for the town of Graceville in far-western Minnesota, the town where her father had grown up and where his parents still lived. Mother was on a summer visit with her grandparents for a week. Since the Jubilee was a historic event, she decided to dress up in Great Auntie Kitty McNally's turn-of-the-century finery. Wearing black from head to toe, she was described as a dark beauty. Her twenty-two-inch waist, plume feather hat, and high-heeled shoes had turned more than a few men's heads at the carnival. One in particular was a tall, dark, and handsome fellow by the name of Evans. He was a *traveler* in the big family of Romanian Gypsies in town to run the Jubilee carnival, and he swept Mother off her feet! Evans brought Mother to the trailer of his sister, who was a palm reader and fortune-teller. The sister took my mother's hand in her own to begin interpreting skin lines and just as quickly released it, saying, "*I cannot read to a power higher than my own.*"

For the next several evenings, Mom snuck out the window of the old Keating house for late-night courting with dark and handsome Evans, until someone caught on. She was quickly sent back home to South Minneapolis to an earful of every evil Gypsy story scare tactic her relations could think of. There had been a marriage proposal from the Evans fellow, and his entire clan got in on the act, offering to crown Mother the queen of the Gypsies if she would only say yes. Their current queen was quite elderly, and word had spread throughout the caravan that my mother, the dark beauty, *had powers greater than* Evans's sister, the fortune-teller, did.

Being accustomed to getting what she wanted, when she wanted it, plans were made to rendezvous at a baby sitting job up the street, where her boyfriend, Tom, agreed to do the actual child care. A glitch occurred when Evans showed up at the wrong home. Mother hid the mix-up by telling her father it was just the Fuller brush salesman at the door. *"Dad was busy punishing Dorothy Gayle, so he didn't notice who it really was."* The way Mom said that part of the story, without skipping a beat, made me wonder if she hadn't been the one who instigated the outburst with her sister.

The rest of this story is one of unrequited love. Mother dumped Mr. Evans, and the last time she heard from him was in an open-faced postcard, on which he wrote, *"I hope your parents never found out you were sneaking out to meet me."* Lucky for her it had been laundry day when that note arrived, and Grandma was too busy to read it. The queen of the Gypsies died that year, but not before putting a hex on Mother's life. *"So, Mom,"* began the question that had haunted my imagination for over four decades. *"What* was *the curse?"* Her reply came without hesitation. *"The curse was that I met your father and married him."*

My parents' marriage was something on the order of an Orwellian nightmare. They had problems that caused us to move a lot. We children experienced prolonged separations from both of them through decades unfolding with episodes of drama and chaos. No one had bothered to offer an explanation of the other curse having its way in the life and DNA of Mother. I don't remember hearing the words *mental illness* spoken out loud back then, only whispers of *"Sherry's got the family curse, the same curse uncle so-and-so died from out at the Willmar hospital."* The *family curse* landed on several of my mother's siblings as well, which gave them permanent addresses in state hospitals. I grew up under the mysterious shadow of this perplexing condition, and it terrified me. Whatever caused my mom to go around town in long underwear—trying to hire a lawyer for purposes of suing the pope—was a powerful thing, one I wished to avoid.

Rituals associated with being a citizen of Catholicism came in handy for surviving curses and other difficulties during my early years. The Holy Sacrament of confession became a strategy to stop the bogeyman from trying to steal my sanity. Kneeling inside an ornately carved wooden box, hands reverently folded, the heartfelt ritual began with *"Father, forgive me for I have sinned."* My admissions to the priest on the other side of the screen were lengthy inventories of every kind of wrongdoing a child could possibly think of. They also were loud enough for the others waiting in line to hear. From time to time a nun would pull me aside with a suggestion of shortening the list of my sins. Once I overheard one say, *"It's as if she carries the world on her shoulders."* I remember thinking they did not understand the gravity of my situation, and I forgave their ignorance of my sacred battle for survival. After all, how could they know that the world on my shoulders was inhabited with devils by the name of schizophrenia, bipolar disorder, violence, and alcoholism? I continued through my Catholic school years this way, repeating earnestly voiced recitations of "Hail Mary full of grace" and "our Father who art in heaven," and performing act after act of contrition. Confessing sins and praying fervently were my spirit weapons to ward off curses and protect me from catching illness in the mind.

Now that I know more about physiology and genetic predisposition for illness, I understand why my relations characterized mental illness with the words *family curse*. When I was a teenager, upon learning of the great hunger and starvation my ancestors experienced, I decided to believe the potato blight was the cause of the biochemical dysfunctions that are a generational plague to the Irish side of my family. I once observed a faith healer pray specifically into the 22nd and 23rd chromosomes in the genetic marker belonging to a person afflicted with schizophrenia. After seeing that, I realized that mother had come by her illness honestly, and that some people are just born *hardwired* for susceptibility to brain disorders.

Down the chronological road, trying to arrange a true and cohesive picture of my childhood for the purpose of writing this book proved a challenge. Something inside of me must have shattered right along with the wedding gift china that exploded on the walls of

112 West 36th Street all those years ago. My puzzle-pieced memories were ceramic shards capable of drawing blood if handled too hastily. Recollections lay scattered in little piles that were nonsensical to my mind's eye. Fitting pieces of shattered memories together required a lot of question asking of relatives whose sharp-edged answers risked cuts into their own wounds of old. Memoir writing in unpleasant lives is a process that takes its time. You need courage and patience, and I recommend finding a good therapist. Reconstructing my childhood was a lot of work, and I'm surprised by how much research was necessary to tell my stories with accuracy.

From questions asked, I learned about the time when my mother's behavior was the most terrifying. It was the year she suffered with undiagnosed trigeminal neuralgia, which is one of the most painful nonfatal medical conditions known to humanity. The trigeminal nerve running across the face hosts shooting pains severe enough to cause suicide and create junkies out of its unfortunate victims. No amount of medication can soothe its burn. Between the maddening pain of Tic-Da-La-Roo, as she called it, and being jacked up on many different pain medications for months on end, her strength became legendary at the county hospital psych ward. I heard she threw six stocky orderlies *and* a piano around upon her admission there. Thank God that someone finally diagnosed her correctly so she could go to the Mayo Clinic for surgery that severed the roots of that nerve. Afterward, one side of her face hung down for years to come, as did her drool, until the nerve would regenerate and she'd need surgery again. We may have inherited a genetic proclivity toward mental illness, but the Ireland in us also bore blessings of resiliency, strength, and restorative powers that enabled one to bounce back from darn near anything—even death—which I was to witness some years later with two of my sons. I came to appreciate a family tradition in which certain difficult situations called for saying, *"You can get an Irishman down, but you can't keep him there long."*

It was my job on occasion to walk over to the Rexall drugstore and pick up Mother's medications. Once the pharmacist had me waiting for half of forever because he was reluctant to fill her prescriptions. I overheard him telling whoever was on the other end of his phone that her meds and their doses were enough to kill a horse. I wanted to tell him that it really was a good thing for my mother to be taking naps all the time. Getting out of the way of a Thorazine shuffle was much easier than the mad scramble of staying one step ahead of manic mood swings. By then my parents had been divorced, and their marriage was well on its way to being annulled by the pope. This dispensation brought mother into good standing with the church and made her a little happier . . . when she was awake.

There had been no furniture big enough for Father to duck behind, and I imagine locking all seven of us behind the bathroom door was impractical and too tight a fit. So, he started hiding out in the bottle . . . and the bars. Eventually, he disappeared altogether into wherever it was that alcoholism took him. I was lonesome for my father and took to wearing his black socks with my Catholic school uniform of green plaid skirt and white shirt. They stretched up to my knees, offering a measure of warmth to legs that had to walk out-side in a Minnesota winter. I didn't know that the little red dimples, marking where his heels should have been, hung off the back of my calves, until classmates laughed and made fun of how it looked. That was not the last time I was to receive attention for unique clothing styles and fashion statements born out of necessity. In the ninth grade I was voted "best dressed" by my peers. What they didn't know is that I had cut up and redesigned the clothing Christian Services brought in big plastic bags to our home every year. We had a Singer sewing machine, and sometimes it worked properly. When it didn't, I snuck in and used the ones in the home economics class to alter and create clothes to my liking.

The aftereffects from growing up as I did showed up in choices of potential mates and in the permissive parenting style used with my own children. As they say, "*If you don't deal with your stuff, it deals with you.*" Despite the best of intentions, I must admit to recreating some of the relational dynamics from my first experiences of learning to give and receive love. Like the moth drawn to flame, I was attracted to addicts and the dreaded personality disorder of narcissism. Addicts in recovery are among the most beautiful, loving, virtuous, and healthy people I have ever been blessed to be in relationship with. I wish I had met my sons' fathers in the recovery stage of their alcoholism. The part of my parenting that suffered was in the key areas of discipline, order, and authority. Not able to differentiate between abuse and discipline, I tried to emulate the laissez-faire style of South Minneapolis hippie families and the culture of *nice* prevalent in realms of middle class—which is who I still thought I was supposed to want to be. Not establishing authority with my children is one of the top three things I would turn the hands of time back to change. It might have helped in coming times of difficulty. All in all, I will sum up my childhood by saying this: What doesn't kill you can mess you up for life or make you stronger and wiser and fetch awards in fashion design.

Both Sides the Twain

My parents named me Julia Kathryn—the Russian spelling of the latter—despite all the Irish blood that went into creating me. Mother had a reason for christening me with that version of my name. It had something to do with her hopes and dreams for little Julia, which included that I would convert all of Russia to Catholicism some day. How do parents come up with such destinies for their children? Needless to say, I did not live up to her expectation of becoming a Catholic missionary, nor did I affect the course of history in the Eastern Bloc. Fate, however, afforded me the opportunity in 1977 to collude ever so slightly in her flight of fantasy regarding my future calling.

I snuck several Bibles into the USSR near the end of the Cold War time, during part of a year spent abroad earning college credit. It was really an undercover pilgrimage intended to transform me magically into a person of the *middle class.* After all, overseas travel-study was essential for all the MBA students with promising futures and very nice teeth. Being a shrewd emulator of all things and people upwardly mobile, I made haste to do the same! Only thing was, the grant I had somehow procured didn't stretch far beyond flying across the ocean to Denmark, where I'd be cooped up with a hotel full of American students for months on end. "*Stupid Americans*" became the refrain heard over and again from the trilingual locals and, as was soon encountered, throughout all of Eastern and Western Europe. I wanted to go to Russia and needed to come up with a *creative financing* plan.

Information garnered from quick and dirty street research included identifying which items of Western origin would fetch the highest price in the black market economy behind the Iron Curtain. With Gideon Bibles borrowed from hotel and motel rooms, bartered-for blue jeans, and Beatles music, my travel plans were soon cemented. I had hot-ticket items and was prepared to parlay said merchandise into luxurious first-class hotels (which was the only class of accommodation available to foreigners at that time) *and* perhaps even travel expenses to my next hoped-for destination—Israel.

The first day in Russia proved to be a navigational challenge for what I had in mind. My inner compass was pointed toward getting out in the mix of everyday people and finding, in particular, Jewish and indigenous Mongolian neighborhoods. I wanted to hear stories about their daily lives and how their communities functioned in caring for one another. At the hotel, tour guides showed up and handed out papers just before the first first-class breakfast was served to our travel group. Daintily proportioned offerings of various shapes, smells, temperatures, and colors arrived on ornately painted china by wide-smiling meal servers dressed up in complicated costumes. I think the beverage glasses were rimmed in gold leaf. All the fine linen and fancy food, combined with the violin virtuoso at each table, set a tone for polite and boring conversation. Oh, was I glad when we got out of there and commenced to see and meet Russia!

We went to beautiful places like jewel-bespeckled subways, big fancy museums, and the Bolshoi Ballet. To my disappointment, we never met or talked with anyone outside the preplanned, tightly scripted excursion. Lunch was back to the fancy-schmancy hotel for more opulent food and limp-as-a-wet-washrag talk about all the pretty things seen on our guided tour. When I asked out loud at lunch, *"Does anyone know where the black market is located?"* the people at my table laughed and said such things as, *"That Julia's such a livewire."* If uncomfortable had a smell, everyone's nostrils would have caught a big whiff of its sour, joy-stifling odor. Such smells trip my inner alarm system. WARNING: You are experiencing social turbulence associated with class privilege! Cascading chemical reactions blushed my cheeks hot red, and urges to curse profusely into their politely laughing faces proved a force almost irresistible. For all the education people of means have, and the amount of value placed on getting it, I'm surprised at how quickly and often ignorance is claimed when it comes to class relations.

My survival issues are not a laughing matter unless and until I say so! Inside my head and heart shame and anger held a carefully guarded conversation on the decibel level of *thought-wave*, although anyone who had passed Body Language 101 could have heard my inner rant. It went something like this. *What the bleep! Let them try to get around all of Europe for a year without Daddy's credit card. . . . I'd like to see that! Y'all wouldn't be so quick to judge if you had to grow up breaking rules, and laws, to survive. Not to say the upper crust never violates the law, because you know darn well you do. It's just that you don't have to sweat like me because you've probably got lawyers on retainer.*

That drama happened many years ago. Little language and even less conversation was available to help me name and understand the complex dynamics unfolding at that dinner table. Now that I am older and have a black-belt degree with such experiences, the rant goes on like this: *Since you like to obtain knowledge so much, I'll give you some. Don't ever be in mixed-class company without it. I want you to know how your polite laughter made me feel all those years ago when I asked about the black market. There was nothing polite about it to me, because your laughter trivialized the energy and struggle it takes to navigate through this world without access to monetary resources. Your laughter felt like an affront and a trespass upon my sacred journey. When you laugh at what I have to do, and how, just to survive in this world, you speak to me about your discomfort, not with me but with yourself, and the insecurity you would feel if ever the tables were turned. That thought probably terrifies you to the bone. Speaking of turning the table, I wish I could watch you walk around for one week in shoes like mine. I'd like to see how far arrogance, ignorance, and knowing it all . . . at all costs . . . all the time . . . would get you.*

This rant could go on for pages, but for now we'll get back to that dinner table. Where was I? Ah yes, pretending not to notice my fellow tourists' pursed lips and stiffening spines, I decided to look at the paper detailing our daily touring schedule to the tune of "Let It Be." It was playing in the ethers between my ears. *"When I find myself in times of trouble, Mother Mary comes to me, singing words of wisdom"* went the lyrics, and I went as well, onto figuring out how to cash in my treasure chest of blue jeans and Bibles!

Mother Mary didn't come to me, but Alexander the elevator attendant did. Perhaps she sent him. Opting to skip the afternoon sightseeing of things and places pretty, I met him on my way up to nap between red satin sheets, upon the four-poster bed, in my five-star room. Their feel was a new pleasure and would surely quell the panic and claustrophobia brought on by glancing at the paper that listed fourteen days of planned touring tedium. Overly structured agendas and me knew one another well by that time. In the previous eighteen years, I had learned fancy footwork to the metered beats of my own creative survival and need for self-care. The two-stepping and jig dancing kept me alive in environmental constructs that did not meet my needs or, worse yet, tried to hinder my growth. Rhythms I heard and moved to throughout my comin'-up years were definitely Irish in nature. Their divinely perfected mathematical configurations were designed with inherent powers to produce joy and a *sure* gift from God. I am deeply thankful that he gave me *ears to hear*, and I am thankful for the resulting joy that became strength enough to survive the many occasions when my dance partner was adversity. It is true and real what Scripture tells us about our joy being our strength! Anyway, let's go back to the elevator. Safely out of earshot and secure behind slammed-shut doors, I spied a new dancing partner who bore no resemblance in any way, shape, or form to adversity, although his name did begin with A. *"Hi, what's your name? Mine is Julia Kathryn, spelled the Russian way even though I'm more Irish than anything else. I come from Minnesota. So, Alexander, do you know anyone who would like to purchase Western clothing and music? I've got several Bibles for sale too!"*

Thanks be to Jesus, Mary the mother of God, and Joseph too! After my date with the satin sheets, and Alexander's elevator shift, we went to his crib (which was about that big). He lived with elderly parents in a two-room flat nestled within a multistory concrete monstrosity. Their home was warm and cozy and didn't have its own bathroom. That was located down a long corridor and was shared by all of the apartment dwellers on their floor! Using cut-up squares of newspaper print for wiping was a new experience. It was stacked ever so neatly. Russians must have had very good plumbing and even better bladder control. I will always cherish the memory of their gracious hospitality—*sposceba* (thank you) and *nastrovia* (to life)!

Thus was the start of Julia Kathryn–style touring of Moscow, Leningrad, and Estonia. It was also the beginning of a growing affection for my middle name and of my desire to be called by such. A very regal *K.* then took up permanent residence between Julia and Dinsmore in my signature. I ended up giving Alexander my guitar, the case of which had cleverly concealed the cache of illegal contraband at customs. It turned out that his greatest desire was to become a Western rock 'n' roll, Beatles-style singer/songwriter/guitar player. Now wasn't that quite a coincidence? It was a big joy for me to be a part of his answered prayer in this way. Plenty more guitars were waiting for me back in the States, but getting hold of just one instrument in the Soviet Bloc at that time was next to impossible. Their all-for-the-group social policy did much to discourage individual artistry. Alexander would have had to purchase every instrument that makes a band just to get one guitar. He and his parents took good care of me, and I had wonderful experiences going on my unsanctioned tours off beaten pathways meeting interesting people, whose conversations were immensely satisfying.

My creative financing plan did not go as expected. Everything I had intended to sell in the underground economy ended up being given away. All worked out well except for the little matter of my not reading the rules that strictly forbade tourists from going anywhere on our own. (I'd only been gone a few days!) I learned later that we were always to stay with our group and could venture out only while in the care of the tour guides. Upon my return to the hotel, the group members I had traveled with were seated on the bus shooting eye-darts my way while awaiting departure to the airport. A large number of official, dark-suit wearing men fanned out around the bus and in the hotel lobby. I heard voices speaking in excited tones of Russian sound-bites, and quicker than John could sign up for the army, they surrounded me with feigning of concern for my well-being. They scrutinized my passport, then rifled through my bags and person as if I was a spy or was trying to steal a precious work of art. After all that, I was asked to get on the bus and invited to leave and never come back. Mother, with her hopes for the conversion of Russia, was crestfallen!

Back in Denmark, I spent time and earned little bits of money in the local folk music scene. One of the regulars at our jam sessions had been diagnosed with cancer while I was in Russia. He passed away shortly thereafter, leaving his considerable collection of instruments to those in our circle of musicians. I received his five-string banjo and taught myself how to frail and strum chords of accompaniment to my singing. Wanting to go to Israel and work on a kibbutz for a few months in exchange for room and board, the next plan for financing plane tickets became my first experience with intentional begging. I sent airmail letters home to everyone I could think of and drew two straight lines through each *s* to look like $. My father had returned from a twenty-year drunk, so I thought it might be a good time to hit him up for back child support he owed from the years we spent living on welfare. Truth be told, I was mightily pissed off with the omnipotent chrome dome (which was what we offspring called his bald-headed self, because that is what Pops looked like while holding court in his new religion of Alcoholics Anonymous). I figured he should pay me for pain and suffering, such as having surgery on my feet from wearing shoes that were too small, and for all the years of babysitting, house cleaning, and other responsibilities an eldest child takes on when a parent is absent. Thanks be to God and the AA program, my father came through. He sent enough money to book the round trip flight to Haifa on the airline of El Al.

Poppy Fields
"One thing you lack: Go your way, sell whatever you have and give to the poor, and you will have treasure in heaven; and come, take up the cross, and follow me."—Mark 10:21

The next leg of my travel-study experience—Israel—had become a reality! To my great fortune, the young woman sitting next to me on that plane was going to work on the very same kibbutz I had signed up for. Our conversations and coming experiences with Polish Holocaust survivors, who founded the community of our destination, became pivotal turning points in my life. God is so good. I thought I was going to Israel to learn about how the remnants of a people could rise from ashes of near total annihilation, to recreate families and build a nation. I wanted to see for myself how a humanity ripped in shreds, could braid itself back together in the aftermath of such trauma. I remember wondering how survivors had managed to retain sanity and love enough for children who came on the cusp of such horrors. I wanted to observe how the kibbutzim organized themselves for young ones to access the collective reservoir of their nurturing and parenting. I thought I was going to see, smell, hear, touch, and taste the source of those things *other people* rely upon to survive atrocities and go on to recover. The Dalai Lama had availed himself of the wisdom of Jewish mothers on our planet in his quest to preserve a culture threatened into extinction by forced diaspora and worse. Now that guy ain't no slouch. If *he* was consulting the Jews about things dear to his heart, curious Julia the social scientist would do the same.

Much to my surprise, the routes I traveled as a social tourist became the road map whose destination took me face-to-face with the country called myself. Myself had been the silent partner, the hidden object of my study of fragmented persons and how they put themselves back together again. I had no idea that the roadways taken to reach others would lead to my coming of age and coming to terms with wounds in my own humanity. Experiences on this travel-study to Israel took up residence in my inner sanctum where things sacred live, which is the reservoir for sourcing the spiritual strength one needs to live in this world.

Some years earlier, my father had given me a compliment. I remembered it because they were few in memory and because I lapped it up like a starving puppy licks a bowl of milk to the last drop and then licks it some more. He had told me, "Julia, you've got really good instincts, good enough to guide you through your life." It turned out he was right about my finely tuned and highly functioning inner bs detector. It proved to be a safety guide through all manner of dangerous situations a *stupid American* could walk in the middle of, while wandering around far from home. Instincts prompted the directions of my travel studies that year, and instincts led to the first hesitant steps of my journey to forgiveness, which was a crag-filled terrain that lay between my father and me. His down payment on back child support was an olive branch to my hostilities from growing up with lack and abandonment. I decided to consider pardoning Father for his long, illicit affair with that greedy, gold-digging, weak-kneed, jelly-backed, jaw-jackin, spineless, pay-check robbing, childhood-stealing, dirty, lying, grave-maker, face-painted, washed-up hussy of a mistress named alcohol. The process of forgiving people who have hurt us is just that, a process. I was ready to take the first step by giving my father a real hug and saying a sincere thank you for making my Israel trip possible when I got home.

It really was disappointing when people back in Minnesota seemed more interested in hearing about Big Ben and the Eiffel Tower than of my interviews with Holocaust survivors and members of the underground resistance movement. They didn't want to know why I wished to learn about human behaviors during the time of Hitler and WWII. No one asked about my desire for answers to questions that had smoldered in my heart like hot lumps of coal since childhood, when first I learned the word *genocide*.

Questions such as:

- How could the entire backbone of a civil society bow down to serve one madman's wicked delusions of exterminating all Jewish people on the planet?
- What made a generation vulnerable to mass brainwashing by the cult of the Third Reich and its doctrine of evil?
- What kind of weakness in the mind allowed people to become convinced by socially sanctioned lies about the existence of such a thing as racial superiority?

- What happened to the humanity of those who were seduced into perpetrating barbaric acts of racial cleansing, and who carried out the final solution in gas chambers?
- What was missing in the spiritual mettle of a culture that it would become accomplice to the commission of mass murder?
- Why did some people allow their neighbors to be carted off to all manner of butchery and certain death?
- Why did others resist this evil?
- Finally, why should all of this matter to us now?

BACK THEN I DIDN'T KNOW HOW TO STRING WORDS TOGETHER ONE letter at a time in printer ink. There was no spell check or using a keyboard. That would have required my brain to rewire itself, which it eventually did, although my thought-hand-eye coordination was stuck in hunt and peck for several years! If it had been possible back then, I would have articulated a term paper about how it was to accompany the young blond-haired, blue-eyed woman sitting next to me on the airplane on our way to the kibbutz in northern Israel. She was an ambassador of a national reconciliation project, and I was bearing witness to a social experiment in healing generational social wounds. I would have told about how terrified she was to be the very first German citizen ever to come to the community of Eine Horasch. Working side by side for several months with Helena and with elders who had survived concentration camps was an amazing experience for the noetic scientist in me. Observing unfolding miracles of forgiveness and redemption while picking oranges, milking cows, and tending chicken coops is the kind of education that stays with you for an eternity. It was also the singular highlight of my sightseeing while overseas! The beauty of forgiveness and mercy being birthed on the kibbutz was in colors I had never seen before. I think one needs spirit eyes to see the nature of that kind of masterpiece.

The oils of that painting had a particular glow, were spectacular, and rivaled the most gorgeous sight I can ever remember, which had been the occasion of seeing

the splendor of fully blooming poppy fields
    in vibrant hues orange and green
dancing graceful movements like the northern lights do
    all the way to horizon's edge.

The poppy fields were views from the bus ride windows as Helena and I made our way to work assignments in the northern parts of the Holy Land. That view took my breath away. The next time I had trouble breathing was the evening we sang together and laughed ourselves silly at a community celebration. I remember strumming my new banjo while leading a humorous made-up-on-the-spot song, "I've been workin' on the kibbutz, all the live-long day." It ended up being the kind of funny where laughter was loud and long, the kind of laughter so hard that you cry and get snotty nosed and have to catch your breath. Waves and waves of laughter crashed over and through the room in repeated undulations that were strong enough to wash away stress and tension. Bliss divine, left in the wake of that emotional cyclone, helped me to understand why some churches practice the art of holy laughing. My term-paper telling would have included the singing of that song, complete with banjo strumming, and would most surely have sealed the deal for fetching a grade of A+!

Those lumps of coal still burn in the heart and are to this day of deep concern to a woman named Julia Kathryn. They have to do with a place in our collective humanity where we are not yet all in agreement about something profoundly key to our existence on earth, and in heaven: that every human life is created in the image of God and is therefore sacred. To this day, my continued and unceasing prayers go up as timber for the upholding of the sanctity and dignity of all human life. I pray strength. I pray strength. *I pray strength* for those who will stand in the gap until we are all of one accord for each person's rightful inheritance to live in the abundance of creation!

Alexander wrote letters from time to time signed, "I Kiss You." I flunked out of college that year and did not return home to the States transformed into a middle-class person. I did, though, have a few more class-disguise props to use for when I wanted to pass—line droppers such as, "*Oh yes, the Austrian Alps were divine to ski, and the mountain chalets were among the finest in Europe."* I also got a look at the books people with good dental plans had, went out and bought them at secondhand stores, filled up my bookcase, and pretended to have read them all!

I got a world-class education that year, one that didn't necessarily make me more employable, and probably less so, but got me well on the way toward obtaining a BA in humanities. Yep, I did eventually get a master's degree in matters of Heart and Soul. Some fine day I hope to become a PhD of Mercy. There are times I wonder if some of my ranting at people with social and economic privilege wasn't displaced anger at my father. I am thinking there is a bit of truth to that. I don't know when or if all these things will sort themselves out completely. I do know this though: harboring unforgiveness does dim and dull the views from bus windows. It obscures our sight and can limit our perceptions in reading road maps. I prefer to see in color and enjoy the adventure of new possibilities that do always appear after each leg traveled on the journey of learning to practice forgiveness, and that's a very good thing!

I Got Up

My coming up wasn't easy, no.
There are periods of time I can't recall.
But certain lines of nursery rhymes
Dwell vividly now that I am grandmother
And early crone, my age approaching five decades.
Their themes of how we all fall down—
"London Bridges" metaphor prepared the child
for when skipping-rope feet caught the crack in sidewalk,
tripped, and skinned her knee. Ashes, ashes,
Grandma lay down, grandpa did too. They never got up again.
They fell. We fall. Bruce says that rhyme is sacred.
I say rhyme is the sound angelic.
There are periods of time I can't recall,
But lyrics in the songs of Mom and Dad
linger in my ear, near where it is that prayers live.
Songs of leaving Ireland behind, of falling in love and from grace.

Their story is medicine parable teacher,
Illustrator of blessings in the storm.
It was a great relief when somebody came
To help put the pieces of Humpty Dumpty back together again, yes,
To the child I was in the age when my coming up wasn't easy.
There are periods of time I can't recall,
But I do remember feeling wanted and needed.
It was a hard life in the age of my early youth,
But I felt that I belonged.
The ground disappeared from beneath my feet with regularity in that time.
Weights and gravity of circumstance knocked me off of my axis of comfort.
Free falls from the balance beam that was emotional gymnastics
    between home and school . . .
Tightrope-walking eldest child act,
    cartwheeling tumbles into the unknown . . . .
Falling, falling, like bridges collapse, like ashes in ring-around-the-
    rosie scatter in the wind, like Rapunzel's hair, like the Berlin Wall,
    like leaves in autumn . . .
like spring rains . . . and everything . . . eventually.
My coming up wasn't easy, no.
But, I'm not sure that I would have kept on keeping on without the
    struggle in my family. Being needed sourced the will and strength it
    took to get up from prone positions as often as I had to. I cherished
    the valuable experience of contributing toward the well-being of
    others. My efforts were valued in return, which gave me the gift of
    depth, meaning, color, and purpose. If we had not known hardship,
    I would not be who I am today, and who I have become is quite all
    right by my standards.
My coming up wasn't easy, no.
But I'm thankful for every good thing that can come from experience.
I'm thankful that I was able to get out of my bed today. I got up.

Sown Seed

To my little Daniel Keating Dinsmore,
Born to me in the wee hours of
December's New Moon.
I love you.

Sown Seed
A son
I loved you before you were born.
Sown Seed
Wee one

I knew you while you were still in my womb.
Water spilling ... Life emerging ...
Opening ... pain ... opening ... push ...
Bath of purification.
You were born.

Sown Seed
Little boy child
It is by you that I know what love is.
You have made me very happy.
Thank you!

Baptism Prayer

Mother's Day, 1983
Son of my own, son of my blood and bone,
You are precious—you are loved.
You are among the fortunate ones
Who do not know hunger.
You have shelter and clothing
And people who will teach you to live.

You are a light—you are hope.
For you know not of bitter things,
Such as jealousy,
Hatred, thieving,
And disrespect to the earth.

You are Lakota—you are Irish.
Baptized Catholic to pennywhistle and drum's beat,
By holy water you were named Eagle Who Soars.
Know your traditions,
For they will give you courage and strength.

I pray for you—take your pride.
Learn to respect yourself.
For it is only then that you will be able
To respect others
And know of the sanctity of life.

Son of my own, son of my blood and bone,
You are precious—you are loved.
Hold this love very closely.
Know this love.
But do not hold it so closely
That you forget to share it with others.

Son of my own, son of my blood and bone,
You are precious.
Love, Mother

Peace Poem

The time for peace is pregnant.
    All the human race is with child,
And soon she will give birth to a new way.
    Every injustice righted,
    Every "I'm better than you" brought to understanding,
Brings us closer to this holy moment.

I say, the time for peace is pregnant.
    All humankind is ripening,
And soon she will harvest a new day.
    Every hatred healed,
    Every mother who has food and hope to feed her young,
Brings nearer to us the sacredness of life.

I say, the time for peace is pregnant.
    All peoples everywhere are joining voices,
And soon they will create a new sound.
    Every injury pardoned,
    Every child who can love with a heart song,
Brings us closer to this holy realization . . .

That the time for peace is pregnant.
    All the human race is with child,
And soon she will give birth to a new way!

I Am the Puppet

I am the puppet,
Waiting for the string to grow shorter,
Filling in the forms until my resistance is dependence.

I am the puppet.
Now my children ask me how to
Fill out the forms of subsistence.
I've earned my freedom!
But still the strings grow shorter.
My children's children stand
In lines to fill out the form
To receive assistance.
The strings grow shorter.

I am the puppet.
Instructions to my daughters—
Know how to fill out those forms,
Stand patiently in those lines,
Teach your children.
I've earned my freedom!

I am the puppet
On a very short string.

I'm a Lot Like You

Chorus: I'm a lot like you. I have needs and you do, too.
There is no conflict here, only what's left if we
Live in fear of each other.

I see you watching me, looking at how I spend my welfare money.
I watch you, dressed so fine, spying on how you spend your time.
You collect antiques, I aluminum cans.
We both like to find things used by other hands.

I live across the street from you, but when we fight
It's as if we're from different lands

Your house is always clean, three meals a day you cook.
The perfect little family, to me that's how it looks.
My house, well, I can't be sure of that.
But like they always say—home is where you're at.
We both like music, be it rock or the symphony.
I sing on my porch, you listen to your CDs;
But when our voices join together
The music we create sets us free.

Our children are spectacular, wonderful, and grand.
The only thing you have that we want is a dad.
My child plays violin best as he can.
Your child rides in a new minivan.
One has music to soothe his soul.
The other has all she needs to get where she will go.
And what each one brings the other . . .
Is all that they know.

Sometimes we're as different as is the night from day.
It's a good thing we can notice that and move along our way.
But when it comes to important things like love and respect,
We draw our bottom line—that's what we expect.
Our lives are like a puzzle, and we each have a part.
The piece we give each other is a piece of our heart.
And that's what's important because
Love's where understanding starts.

Food Stories

The Lord's Diner

I have the opportunity to visit many towns and cities in the
Upper Midwest and around our nation for the purpose of assisting citizen leaders to plan strategies to combat social and economic

disparity. Sometimes my stay lasts a duration of hours; other times I'm engaged in dialogue and performance for as long as ten days. Each of these ending poverty road trips is interesting and a uniquely pleasurable experience. The noetic scientist in my heart delights to see with my own eyes good people and efforts in change making. Yes, every community is different. Yet I have come to expect a particular joy, like a child's eager anticipation of presents under the Christmas tree. It happens as regular as rush hour. Someone is always operating a ministry, new community action program, or social justice effort that he or she is passionate about. The reason for the excitement and pride is usually that the work bears fruit or the promise of such. Peoples' lives are changing in good ways or the community's health is improving. Sometimes the flow of wealth has increased in a place. One thing's for sure: I can report that our country is full to brimming with social capital and dynamic assets of the human kind! It is an inspiration to observe the diversity of solution-seeking initiatives and creative social ideas that citizens employ to engage a problem that has plagued humanity for so long.

One example of citizens being their neighbor's keeper is located in Wichita, Kansas. It happens to be a feeding ministry, and this section of my book is about food, so y'all are going to hear about the Lord's Diner. I generally like to keep an eye out for promising social ventures that are on the systemic change tip. Until the day comes when we decide to distribute wealth and resources fairly, hungry and homeless people will be among us. In the meantime, the practices that extend care to dispossessed citizenry can stand some improving. The Lord's Diner is a service-based project that lit up my hope radar. Its concept can be replicated easily, and I hope to hear of diners springing up in other places.

Somebody came up with the idea to create a buffet-style restaurant that would stay open 365 days a year and serve quality meals that are affordable to the homeless and hungry. The cost? *No Charge*. And how does Wichita do this? It is a lesson in community capacity building in a most lovely way. Money was raised to build the restaurant from the usual funding sources. Interdenominational faith communities contribute money every month to purchase food and pay utility bills. Chefs from surrounding country clubs and dining establishments donate their labor on a regularly revolving schedule to provide lively menus every day of the week. The building was designed and decorated with the social ambience of any other family-style buffet eatery.

Anyone can come to the Lord's Diner and eat a meal in an atmosphere that has reduced the monolithic divides between the classes. You don't have to be poor to dine there! Your money is most welcome, as is the pleasure of your company. We may not have opportunities to spend time with *all* of our neighbors, considering the rapidly stratifying structural confines in this day and time. Breaking bread together is sacred common ground where possibilities exist for our reclamation of one another. The beauty and brilliance of the Lord's Diner is that it is not the one-way street of *I am here, serving you*. No, it is a two-lane roadway on which we may greet and meet and eat with each other. It is a place with a theme of *we are strangers no more*.

Lastly, I will note that the effort to uphold human dignity within this concept of food ministry is not to be underestimated. It may sound like a trivial afterthought to consider social atmosphere when talking about something as basic as the need to eat. Well, I'm here to tell everyone that any attempt to preserve the dignity of those of us suffering under lack is far from trivial. The mean-spirited circumstances, systems, and, yes, people that we encounter daily are a huge burden. For many of us, hope has grown dim that our personal station in this world ever will improve.

Realms intangible may seem less real to persons who experience the regular comfort of meeting basic needs. People without material accoutrements, however, vividly perceive these realms. They are the source of company and compassion in an uncaring society. We are very sensitive to the atmosphere in the ethers. We recognize Christ immediately. The temperature of love and kindness in realms intangible is warm. We feel it in the God thermometer that has become a highly refined instrument in our bodies and souls. So, the little ways of uplifting human dignity are not so little after all. Basic human respect is very meaningful to all people, but especially to those for whom this measure may be the only nourishment in their day. I say yes and yes again for the Lord's Diner!

The Extra Plate

During the years of my sons' childhood in the Twin Cities, our food budget consisted of an assortment of programs, food shelves, feeding ministries, and bulk buying clubs. Stay-at-home moms were becoming extinct at that time, so many of us can say that we raised our own kids . . . and half the neighborhood! Since afterschool programs were scarce and waiting lists for child-care assistance were five-years long, latchkey kids were abundant. Children are good little survivors. They know which of their friends has a parent at home and food in the fridge. It was a rare day when there weren't extra mouths in the house. By the time rent and utilities were paid, not much was left of our AFDC check. Most of poor people's income is spent for rent, so I was surprised that landlords didn't form their own advocacy group and lobby the legislature to keep our checks coming during the time of welfare reform! The $169 in food stamps our family of four qualified to receive never stretched through the entire month, so my food routines became a hodgepodge of experiences marked by two things: Getting food was time consuming, and doing so always involved interactions with community. The leaning-on relationship, in ways mutually beneficial, was a sweet song and joy-filled accompaniment of my child-raising years.

One year I won the McKnight Foundation Virginia Binger Outstanding Minnesotan Award. It came with a $5,000 check, and the first thing I did when it cleared was take my children to the big food store in our neighborhood. They each got their own shopping cart, and they filled them to overflowing with food and food more. They strutted around the store like proud peacocks, like we had just won the lottery, like poor folk . . . whose wealth and daily security is measured by fullness in the cupboard. They pushed those carts with heads held so high I thought their necks might strain their muscles. Their eyes didn't see where to steer and bumped into displays, aisle dividers, and other people. I think the boys wanted others to notice us, show some respect, and pay homage to how rich we were. I chuckled at the sight of them flaunting their entitlement to boxes of Fruit Loops and Frosted Flakes in quantities they had never known before. Their little shoulders swaggered back and forth with each

sure-footed step, prestige of wealth tried on for size and feel, pushing cart their very own. Isaac even had to stop and tie his shoe, as
sloppy shoelaces didn't go at all with the class of his shopping cart.
"Say, sir, can you help me find the frozen White Castle hamburgers?
. . . I'll take ten boxes, with cheese!" And "Excuse me again, what
direction is the snack food aisle?" I laughed out loud when English
accents spouted from their tongues and harder still upon hearing
new manners appear in dialect of royalty. I laughed so long and hard
my belly ached for days.

The other children at the store that day provided more humor,
with mouths agape in wide-eyed amazement at the stupefying sight of
us shopping to our heart's delight. Had I caught on movie camera the
scenes of people stopping in their tracks, with looks of bewilderment
on their faces, we could have contended for *America's Funniest Home
Videos*! Oh, the joy was sweet and unique and better than watching
them open Christmas and birthday presents. The other shoppers that
day probably thought we were from a group home, out purchasing
the month's supplies. Come to think of it, our house was a group
home . . . without a budget, though, except for the McKnight award.
If someone ever decides to make a movie on my life, make sure this
event makes the final cut, okay? The grocery store shopping spree is
the happiest memory in my parenthood's entirety—that is, after the
incomparable thrill that was the first beholding sight of babies newly
born to me.

The community of my survival was, by and large, a diverse network of welfare moms and dads engaged in activities of daily living
that keep parents busy. Sharing was the unspoken bylaw, and practic-
ing generosity, the dues for belonging to our unorganized, highly
functioning patchwork quilt of mutual assistance. When a family
of six showed up to your door at mealtime, there was no need for
uncomfortable conversation about how hungry the children were.
We didn't have forms to fill out or make people provide proof of
their income, how and what they had spent it on, or the identity of
their national origin. The Irish have a custom called "setting the extra
plate" at the table, as one never knows when Jesus will be coming
for dinner. I have been blessed by experiences of living with lack, for

poverty was the table upon which the extra plate could be placed
. . . regularly. The cloth underneath may have been ragged, but the
food from realms intangible nourished much more than the body.
Opportunities to experience the gift of generosity, in giving *and*
receiving, were boundless and enriched my family life in many ways.
I am thankful for the teachings that come from adversity and hunger.
I have also gained an appreciation for the transformative spiritual
practice of fasting and understand more fully why so many of the
world's religions engage its discipline.

I learned the most regarding generosity and food from native
people. When I think about how much was stolen from the Anishi-
nabe and Lakota people, seeing them share anything at all—let
alone their food, which was often the *only* thing they had—well,
that was a staggering sight, something you never forget! My children grew up attending the many community celebrations, pow-
wows, ceremonies, fry-bread taco sales, and memorials held in
the Indian country of South Minneapolis. Many of these occasions
called for a feast, and someone would put a spirit plate out by the
base of a tree or in another special spot to feed the ancestors. Seeing this practice reminded me of my own family tradition with the
extra plate, and I realized we had more in common than I'd previously thought.

Friends taught me their tricks and particular zing for making
hangover soup and commodity stew. I shared Irish dishes, such as the
recipe for *hair of the dog that bit ya the night before*—which called for
a whiskey before breakfast chaser—and Mrs. Murphy's Chowder.
Amazing thing was, the ingredients needed for our respective cultural delicacies were exactly the same—imagination and whatever it
was that happened to be in the cupboard and icebox on that day! Mac
and cheese was a staple for nearly every meal, as commodity cheese
was given out every month in large bricks. Waiting in the commode
lines was always an adventure and fun because it was a chance to
catch up on the news in one another's lives. Good humor was abundant, and needed. Shaking with laughter got our blood circulating
enough to keep toes from freezing in the months of bitter cold Minnesota winters of old. Before global warming.

The neighborhood was full of people who lived their lives in a spirit of openhandedness, which I did not witness again until years later on occasions of being in the midst of native Hawaiians and aboriginal Australians. Wow! The way generosity dwells inside indigenous peoples is immediately recognizable and of great beauty to me. Generosity must be a powerful spirit, because it lives so fully in these most-hurting people on the planet. It illuminates their words and ways with a glow precious and rare, one I am deeply thankful to have been in the presence of. I used the word *openhandedness* earlier in this paragraph, and the thought occurred to me to wonder where the statement of *being caught red-handed* originated and how it could possibly have meant anything derogatory. It should be a great compliment of honor and respect for the spirit of fellowship and sharing I have always found in first nation people.

Beyond sharing food, cultivating a patient spirit was of utmost importance in the life of a welfare mother. Eliza was my role model when it came to patience. If I remember correctly, she had about nine or ten children of her own, and dozens of grands, cousins, nieces, and nephews were always nearby, if not underfoot. Her big heart loved on the women in our group who were newly poor through steady, precise word and story.

Eliza Sings

Her listening ears and watchful eyes were a ministry to the community.
Her grandmother voice was rich and warm like a blanket, like a shawl.
It resonated in tone of drum, with instructions to those not familiar with
*   where to find clothes, housing, and the complicated, expensive routines of*
*   eradicating head lice. Her voice showed us how.*
In meters slow, wisdom like honey poured between the spaces of she and we,
*   just as lava flows. Her instructions floated on lamentation's aire, lingered*
*   her voice did, lavished us with what we didn't know we needed. She knew.*
Her speed was slow. It was the color of middle blue.
Her melody was velvet on the skin of cheeks, soaked up tears that ran when
*   they needed to. Middle blue rubbed on the complexion of my worries, velvet*
*   words. Soothed.*
Our friendship like velvet was soft, was gentle, was patient, was not haughty or
*   hard like the world is. She liked her Pepsi.*

Survival sermons sounded eloquently between sips and a smoke on the porch,
*   behind cedar trees.*
Cedar stood guard where we hid from children many.
*   We hid from the next crisis, the next fire, the next shut-off notice, the next*
*   death, behind in rent, and the death after that.*
Death came in twos and threes every month, sometimes weekly.
The next funeral always came the same but differently. She sang. At home-
*   goings. Recently departed loved ones in family and community, frequent*
*   flyers club.*
Membership of colonization's remnant, ravaging,
*   raped by eminent domain, derelict insane, depravity.*
It was Wasitu who was savage, still is. It was genocide. Is stilling many voices.
Eliza's voice is alive. She sings to children,
*   and the newly arrived to poverty's door, and Auntie Margaret.*
At the door in the shaking wigwam, opens doors. Marked Ojibwa. She sings.
Dear Eliza on the porch, at feasts singing things into Daniel, my son.
He couldn't sing in pitch Western, but sitting at the drum his voice
*   was ancestral. It was.*
On key. Melody of Eliza, of the song recognizable. He sang. Unashamed.
Learned song in rhythm slow to judge, and pride that is not style European.
*   Not false. Pride in generosity and patience. Pride the color middle blue.*
Not pride puffed up on itself, but soft like velvet on cheek. Wipe tears.
Like wind in the tall grass, like Daniel's grass dance, in rhythm slow to anger.
Eliza sings. Eliza at the door open.

ELIZA SPOKE IN SPEED SLOW TO JUDGE WHEN NEWCOMERS
vociferously protested, boo-hooed, and complained about having to
do things that were beneath their dignity—like use food stamps in a
public place (the grocery store) where God and the next door neighbor might see—or worse, eat at Loaves and Fishes in the basement of
Holy Rosary Church. We had long been accustomed to the multitude
of skin pricks that are daily interactions with our environment. In
time one learns it is not humanly possible to defend dignity against
every demeaning assault encountered in the territory of America's
underclass. In time one learns to save energy for *real problems,* which
were plentiful and always around the next corner. We had learned

to make jokes about the absurdities that dropped into our days like unwanted guests who overstay their welcome. On more than one occasion, there was a bomb threat at the Ramar Building on Franklin Avenue. After spending an hour or more in the food-stamp line, I had to leave with no way to feed my sons. Now that was a problem! Good humor is one of the survival skills hard-pressed peoples use in ample proportions. In time, those who were newly arrived to the community of the absurd learned to laugh more. Yes.

Laughter as Food

Communities from ranks of generational poverty have long known about the pharmaceutical capabilities in human biochemistry. Laughter is our Prozac. It also serves as our escape and as a source of affordable entertainment.

Laughter comes in handy in many different applications. Those who have skill in finessing humor's transformative powers can get elevated to status of shamanistic respect in the community of the down under who are hard-pressed. The fool? I don't think so. I have witnessed humor's use in conflict resolution and in domestic abuse flare-ups, both of which are deadly and are all too common where we live. Before state programs of economic assistance, child support, and food stamps became electronically transacted with EBT cards (and before financial workers' jobs were outsourced to overseas), mail carriers delivered checks to our mailboxes. Now with all the moving that we do, can you imagine what those unfortunate carriers went through? Hell at times, I'm quite sure.

Once I relocated four houses down on the same block.
The bureaucracy had a terrible time processing my new address,
    and my assistance got lost for two weeks. Nearly evicted.
I waited with bated breath each day at half past two, when the mail was due.
    I rearranged the schedule of my schooling to be there. I nearly pulled my
    hair out with frustration. I got to know my mail carrier by his first name.
I was told he wanted battle pay, and how he never left on his route without the
    mace.
His face was the only one available for venting of our rage.

We often engage with faceless systems, which don't always work right.
We get very frustrated, and there are times when we snap.
Most of the time we take out our frustrations on ourselves. We medicate.
Sometimes we take things out on our families. This we hate.
Other times we snap on whoever happens to cross our path, at the wrong time.
　　We leak. On many occasions one of us went postal on the post person.
　　Charged
and convicted. We were maced in the face.
Disgraced in front of the neighbors and the kids who were
home from school. Absent again. The children were hungry.
They usually eat two meals in the cafeteria at school. They were waiting
for the check to arrive. So that head lice medication could be bought.
So the cab fare to the laundromat could be paid, to kill lice.
　　They were waiting.
For their check. So that back to school they could go. But no. This particular prob-
　　lem happened on the block where we lived in South Minneapolis. Desperate.
Mother hauled to jail. Children all went into foster care. They did.
And so did the check. It arrived the very next day. Too late. Too bad for them.
　　So sad.
If only Melvin had been around.
He calmed someone down with the very same issue a time before this one. It
　　was blissful to witness this situation. Serious consequences he diffused.
Humor was used. Everyone laughed and nobody went to jail.
All hail.
Ecosystems of people are delicate. Tenuous at best.
We don't get our rest. We're tired, and weary, and trying to do our best.
　　To survive.
Each new day brings trials and tribulations, complications,
　　rearranging time and energy to face the next crises. We try.
Our best to minimize stress deadly. Flares up.
Our consequences are hard, and big, and heavy. Weighs us down.
Our burdens weigh heavily.
Bender of backs
　　causes sight to light upon the ground of our own footsteps. We stop.
　　Looking people in the eye. Looking life in the eye. Eyesight no
　　longer on the prize.

We do the best we can under the circumstances,
    under their weight. We do the best that we can every day.
We're really amazing. We don't go postal more often. Thank the Lord—
A tribute to our sanity,
    retaining humanity, ability. Agility retained our humor. We laugh. Holy
    laughter.
Melvin makes medicine on the block. It is amazing. It is.
It is Melvin hanging a shingle on the door he does not have.
Did you laugh at that? You have my permission. To laugh with us. Not at us.
Just don't laugh too loud at certain times.
You'll get the hang of our humor with a quickness. It'll catch.
At the laughing club I wish to start.
I would employ Melvin as the ringmaster.
He could have his very own door. A sign.
Would read Dr. of Hilarious Divinity,
Laughter Therapist,
Conflict Resolution Specialist.
He could make a lot of money with his skills,
Run anger management classes if the felony on his record gets removed.
Melvin makes medicine in the community.
Wounds heal. Wounds prevented. Hope invented. Melvin makes medicine in the
    community.
We laugh.

Kindness at the Food Shelf

My circle of friends operated like a refugee resettlement council. Most of us had several generations of poverty living under our belts, and we served as a safety net of sorts for the next family to come our way. The downwardly mobile first-timers on welfare, more often than not, still had a car in working condition. We veterans would spend time teaching them how to be poor on the way to the food shelf. Showing of the ropes included many instructions. Here's how you get to this food shelf, don't forget all the legal identifications for every child, and so forth. We'd cram more people into those cars than was legal. We began entertaining ourselves with adventures in *drive-by laughing* on our outings. My brother had just been a victim of a gang initiation drive-by shooting while walking to the store in the Seward neighborhood. Thanks be to the Almighty and to the saints, his life was spared. It was quite a scare, as he could have died when the bullet hit his femoral artery. Driving around laughing uncontrollably in a car too full of people had a medicinal effect on my sons and me after my dear brother was shot. Yes. We laughed. HA! Into the face of death and danger, and spread much happiness on the South Side that year.

Thus was the routine of getting to food shelves for the monthly allotment, which, if you were especially crafty, could be prepared in such a way as to last three and a half days. Sometimes people who worked at the food pantries (usually women) were cold and hard. Sometimes the most mean-spirited of them acted that way because once upon a time they had been *us*. They had gotten a job, so what was our excuse for being hungry? I always tried to stand in the line headed by the nice church ladies who hadn't lived hard-luck lives. They wore knit sweaters with covered buttons and still had all their own teeth, which could explain the easy, genuine smiles breaking upon their faces, which I did appreciate and still do.

Poverty's face, after a time can resemble stone-etched profiles,
Can appear harsh, and hardened.
Poverty's face hasn't seen a dentist in half of forever.
We're not trying to act mean and sullen,
It's just that we don't always smile in mixed company.

The aversion of our glance is not meant to insult.
Eyes darting here and there are looking for a place where invisible can exist
    for just a moment,
The moment when we want to disappear because of fear. And shame.
Because of knowing judgment's pain, and feelings that have many other
    names.
It's too much to contain. We look down, where invisible can exist for a moment.
That pregnant moment, my mortality miscarried many little deaths that
    Occurred in little moments, in glances.
In a look someone gave to me once upon a time. Just after the age when,
I was young. When my delighting eyes searched hungrily, expectantly
    For reflection, attention, and mutual love without condition.
When my eyes exuberant waited patiently for connection, protection, and comfort.
When joy was looking at the eyes that were looking back at mine.
When disappointment was delight dimming,
    Was when eyes tired, dull, devoid of love to behold, were looking back at me.
When there was no one looking after me eventually.
When curious, joyful, trusting, innocent, wonder-filled child eyes began to
    realize.
    People stop looking at one another somewhere along the line.
Then it became dangerous to look at people in their eyes, in the neighborhood.
You could get shot. This is true.
    Ask my brother. Go ask around the block.
Chance meetings in eyes. Don't get caught gazing for too long.
It was just a glance, the chance it could be fatal, how it felt.
    It was just a feeling.
What is the true nature of a smile, and how long is the length of a while?
What is special in the moment of a glance
When eyes earliest acquaintance do impressions make?
When just a moment is a glimmer in time, it shines.
That glance becomes the chances that we take.
When a glance is the moment, becomes a gaze amazing.
Windows on souls, our eyes. My face, your smile, we gaze.
We glance; we take the chance, to gaze through the glass of the window.
In the moment of a glance when eyes' earliest acquaintance do impressions
    make.

When a glance can last for eternity.
When a chance not taken is eternity lost, forever.
When I am afraid to be seen.
When I am afraid of seeing that which I fear.
    When possibility approximating exists
            To catch a glimpse of the reflection
                    That we are.
The chance we take.
Windows on souls,
    our eyes.
        My face,
                your smile,
                        we gazed.
When a glance, became the window, is the gaze,
    became a mirror.
Is the reflection
    That we are.
Because I needed to be valued.
Because your countenance deserved to be acknowledged.
Because possibility approximating exists,
    In moments.
        In a glance.

Living treasure? It is well-being inspired by recalling experiences of meeting another's eyes. Gazing at the beauty of expression in those I have known is a joy. Their unique look and sound and feel, the way their glasses set upon the face and nose, and best of all was kindness at the food shelf. Encountering kindness thoroughly and often is good for the prevention of hardened heart and prickly aura. Bumping into the presence of kind hands and kind words helped us make it through the parent-bashing social climate of welfare reform. Contemplating those lovely blue-haired church ladies with nice teeth who parceled up meals so long ago, I am struck by how vibrantly they remain in my memory. I can still see their comfortable smiles clearly. They are living treasures. They sparkle.

Oh, Little One

Oh, little one, inside of me—
What kind of a world are you gonna see?
Will you look with shock and disbelief,
Or turn your head from others' grief?
What will you think of the rich ones
Who protect their power with tanks and guns?
Will you stand? Will you fight
When you're taught that white is right?
Oh, little one, . . . *Will you fight?*

Oh, little one, what's in store—
In a city full of sirens waging a poverty war,
Where people steal from one another,
From their sister, from their brother,
Where there's rules that the state arranges,
That the poor must endure and the rich can change?
Will you rise? Will you speak
When a woman-loving woman's not allowed to teach?
Oh, little one, . . . *Will you speak?*

Oh, little one, I hope you'll care—
For the earth's great waters, for birds and clean air.
Will you believe people's promise of progress and might
While they're raping the earth and making a plight?
Will you realize when the sky rearranges its hue
That with trees and four-leggeds you're nature too?
Will you sadden? Will you cry
Should the ancient forests give up and die?
Oh, little one, . . . *Will you cry?*

Oh, little one, inside of me—
What kind of a world are you gonna see?
Will you find loving people to see you through?
And find out what it is you must do?
Will you learn to have faith in good powers unseen,

In the wonder of mountains and water serene?
Will you laugh? Will you delight
In the hopes and dreams of a better life
Oh, little one, . . . *Will you delight?*

Blame & Shame

I MET A SOCIOLOGIST AT ST. MARY'S COLLEGE in San Jose, California, while on a performance/educational residency in their Service Learning department. She spoke to something that stays in my conscious thoughts to this day, even though it has been a good eight years since I heard her words. This woman, originally from Italy, had spent most of her life in countries other than the United States, including places that many refer to as the Third World. *She said she'd never seen a culture blame and shame its poor like we do in America!* It seems to me that the blame the victim game is one of the oldest tricks in history's toolbox for use in maintaining the status quo. I think our national tolerance for social and economic policy that benefits small numbers of people disproportionately is rooted in this blame and shame.

I can't remember her name, but to this woman I will always be grateful. You see, her insight allowed me to stop faulting myself for

- not being smart enough to get a college education.
- not being organized or strong enough to work two or three jobs at a time.
- not being able to bear the workload of two parents or an extended family as a single parent.
- not being good or industrious enough to deserve adequate housing, a safe neighborhood, or quality schools for my sons.
- not feeling worthy enough to receive needed medical or dental care.

Thank you, Ms. Sociology Teacher. By your spoken observations I began to understand how our nation's affordable housing crisis factored into why we had to move so many times. I began to understand that the children's mental health systems were set up, more often than not, to enrich themselves rather than preserve my family or my child's health.

Bless you, Ms. Lady Not from Here. You interrupted the daily conversation between my ears that went something like this: *What is wrong with you, Julia? You can't even figure out how to earn income enough to support three sons? You must be doing something terribly wrong!* The truth told is that all my time and energy was consumed by being an unpaid psychiatric technician to two sons with brain injuries in my home. I didn't even have time to sleep, or did so with one eye open for years!

Oh, the weight that was lifted upon realizing that crowded therapeutic foster homes were being paid from $1,200 to $3,000 a month to care for my child. So, it wasn't a case of bad parenting by me after all, and Freud's mother-blaming theories were not necessarily true!

Foster parents got social and economic supports to which I was denied access. Hmmmmm . . . It was also a tremendous relief to figure out that bad parenting was not the cause for my sons' experience of failure in school. Instead, it might have been more the case of schools failing my sons, when districts were expected to carry out *unfunded federal mandates* like the No Child Left Behind Act. Thank you, thank you, to that woman who studies and instructs on how we think about and set up our communities. Your sharing ushered the spirit of liberation into my being!

In this land, holding people entirely responsible for not achieving the American Dream, or, at the very least, not surpassing the economic station of their parents, seems to be a practice with a long history. It is a persistent and pervasive cultural practice, deeply embedded within our national identity. I do not care for its odor. To me, it carries the stench of ill health, similar to how end-stage cancer smells.

Who does it serve?
and
Who does it harm?

It is true that cities and townships across America have more families than homes to house them. So why does the notion persist that people are homeless because they want to be . . . and that living in streets, under bridges, and in shelters is their preference? It is disconcerting to me that the mythology of *homeless by choice* is alive and well today. It all too commonly surfaces in dialogue I've experienced with countless college students over the course of twenty years.

Blaming the homeless for their plight prevents us from acknowledging the simple fact that our nation's affordable housing stock is not keeping up with the needs of its citizens. It saddens me that I've been waiting in vain to hear these questions from university students:

- What happened to the tenants of Cabrini Green, Robert Taylor Homes, and other public housing high-rises when they were torn down?
- If only a small fraction of those housing units were replaced, where did all the families go?
- Why do we spend so much money on transitional housing? What is there to transition to?
- How many resources are poured into paying for months on end at motels and shelters?
- Why does the state of Minnesota spend more on HMIS (the paper trail for keeping track of the homeless) than is spent on our entire transitional housing budget?
- Why are we not investing resources in permanent affordable housing?

Instead of hearing questions that come from being well informed, students say that poor people just don't know how to budget their money, or that they use their income for drugs, alcohol, and elaborate televisions instead of paying their rent or saving for down payments on homes. Stereotypical accounts still abound regarding people in public housing who don't work, engage in criminal activity, and just get high and party all the time. I want to tell these future social workers, teachers, city planners, business administrators, and lawyers that

- most cities in America have waiting lists for subsidized housing that are so long, only one day of the year is set aside just to apply. The wait can be up to a decade long!
- enduring the wait is spent by many people on endless routines of shelter hopping or couch surfing in friends' and relatives' living rooms.
- most public and privately owned slum housing is in dire need of repair. Running water can be a seasonal occurrence. Hot running water is a luxury. The funky atmosphere of overcrowded dwellings, where meeting personal hygiene and clean clothes is not guaranteed but flaring tempers are, could drive a person to drink . . . or worse after a while.

I want to hear discussion at universities and churches about

- how persons with drug convictions are not eligible to reside in subsidized housing.
- how prison recidivism rates correlate with housing availability.
- how addiction in America is no stranger to the well heeled.
- how it is all right for our leaders' families to have drinking and addiction issues while residing in the White House, yet they still get to stay in their public housing.

I have yet to hear meaningful dialogue about the following:

- the United States has more citizens caught up in the penal system then any other nation on the planet.
- those who determine the future need for prison beds in America gauge their calculations by reading scores of third graders.
- How many unfortunate members of our prison population could have avoided such a fate if their parents had access to more caring societal constructs, such as
  - an economic system that is compatible with full employment of its citizens.

- affordable permanent housing instead of homeless shelters.
- comprehensive medical care instead of foster homes.
- a guaranteed minimum income instead of a poverty and prison industrial complex.

In closing this essay on fault-finding, I am compelled to think of my children. I wonder how much self-blame they have internalized for how their lives turned out. Would it make a difference for them to know that our society planned to spend resources on building them a prison cell rather then invest in meeting their basic needs when they failed third-grade reading? I ask myself, *Would they still be living on the streets and in and out of institutions if comprehensive medical care had been available that included in-home supports for children with mental health and bio-brain disorders?*

It's not useful for any of us to perpetuate the blame game. Doing so only causes more wounds to those who already bear the burdens of social and economic unfairness. I think it is useful, however, for us as a society to take responsibility for the harm done to people who have historically suffered or currently suffer under lack. We should address generational hurts that began in slavery and the colonization of North America. We need to acknowledge the fact that the labor of many, many people was ripped off to benefit a few.

If we must place blame, why not start with looking at systems, public policy, and structures that control the flow of wealth and resources in our nation and world? If there is any use for shame, then let it move all of us whose basic needs are met toward truth, reconciliation, and rectifying resources to a new bottom line . . . the bottom line spelled H-U-M-A-N-I-T-Y!

Let shame—if it is possible—mobilize our collective desire to do better by ourselves by creating a land where every person can eat and live in a safe community. If anything good can come of shame, then I say, shame on us! Let its sting help us avoid greed and false beliefs of entitlement to more than our fair share of earth's abundance. Let it be motivation to build more housing and fewer jails. Let it build more families and fewer foster homes. Let it spark an outpouring of more treatment and a cure for AIDS instead of AIDS orphanages. Let shame be the moral compass that guides us through honest inventory taking of our social shortcomings. Finally, then, let it show us exactly what is expected from those of us to whom much has been given!

I dedicate the following song to my children and to anyone coming out of the shackles of undeserved blame and the immobilizing, shame-shrouded aftermath of wrongful accusations.

"And we know all things work together for good to those who love God, to those who are called according to His purpose."—Romans 8:28

Part B. There Were Rainbows Somewhere over Our Sorrow

By Grace Go I

You see torn and tattered.
I see threads of life worn.
You hear ta-boom music too loud.
I hear the pulse of creation.
You say—get a job, earn a living.
I say—my living is my job.

Chorus: And by grace go I through the night,
            And by grace that I might have sight
            To see the things I see.

You see unkempt and not cared for.
I see no need for charades.
You say—pay your rent but don't live here.
I say—the fingerprints look just fine on the door.
You feel your belt tighten and look with that stare,
But I feel it much more.

You say—black sheep and crazy.
I say—breaker of yokes
You see the things you're afraid of.
I see a glimpse of hope.
And all the time and trouble spent trying to be blind
Are just my sense of protection as I walk through this dangerous time.

Reclaiming Working-Class Men

Laughs loudly, sings with heart of passion,
not too proud to show your tears
and known to cuss.
Not too much pretense in you.
People always know where they stand with you,
because black is black and white is white and
they better work hard for God, family, and country.
Politically incorrect as can be, rigid and fiercely loyal to the practical values
of living, sometimes to the point of closed-mindedness.
But not so with matters of the heart.
That big working-class heart,
with its generosity and emotional honesty,
shows salt of the earth care and concern
For family, neighbors, and the little ones
who ride their bikes up and down the alley.

Flagpole in your yard, your pride is more than flapping in the wind. You live your convictions—head, heart, and hand seem connected. You work in your toolshed out back, making things out of throwaways and fixing anything and everything. Strategically so, because out back with the big garage door open you keep pulse with the doings and community around you, keep the connection to people alive, while your sons in their own homes sit in their little dens with their uncalloused hands dancing on the computer keyboard . . .

In isolation. Did you want for your sons to be able to "buy new" and get a comfortable white-collar life? I like you better. I like the grumpy old men in the city who tend their lawns and shrubs ad nauseam. They know how to fix my cupboard door and will do so. How many times, Bob, did you get my car running in the dead of a Minnesota freeze? The homemade rubber-band shooters you gave were my kids' favorite Christmas gift for years.

Yeah, you can be a son of a gun. You hold a grudge for half of forever—didn't talk to Don Pederson down the block for fifteen years. Lenny next door looked into your casket with eyes that seemed to regret that you two weren't on speaking terms the last time you went to the hospital. How about the time you threatened to saw my basketball hoop pole in half because all the neighborhood kids were too loud out your bedroom window? I said I'd give you a dime to call my landlord, and then you really started spewing obscenities. Flailing arms and pointed finger raged in my face, and your wife came out to calm you down.

I am honored to have tangled with you, because I think you knew you were leaving soon, and saying goodbye would have been too much, too, too heartbreaking. I get it, Bob. I avoid goodbyes too. Thanks for giving us neighbors seeds from the angel plants in your garden. Thirty-some years you watched over this corner of Minneapolis. Your flowers are still growing. It felt so big to me when you died, as if a wonderful piece of working-class culture went to the grave with you. Who will keep the traditions of heart alive?

Who will be the new keepers of connection? This upcoming generation of elders seems too disjointed to me. Who can I have a good fight with? People don't know how to get mad at each other today without getting a gun. Whatever happened to the good old fist fight? People either kill each other or do the passive aggressive thing. Yes, anger, working-class anger, hot, to the point, in your face, honest, righteous indignation, cuts to the quick, making clear to me how much love there is behind the blustering. Clear to me how much of your anger and raging are rooted in your great love for humanity. How much of your labor was exploited so someone else's kids could get fat and lay by their swimming pool?

Even through the worst, those damned bloody wars you fought, you came back to your VFW halls and did good in your communities. I love the VFW bingo halls, but they're all "For Sale." Proceeds from them keep the Little Leaguers in T-shirts. They supply wrestling mats on the floor at the park gym and buy football equipment. Working-class traditions like volunteering to coach sports for twenty years in a row are disappearing. Nowadays, men and women think they have to write a grant to pick up a bat and ball and play with children at the park.

Working-class culture is alive and well in VFWs, where friendships have lasted decades and the neighborhood folks play their quarters—young, old, black, white, native, Hispanic, come together in a good way. That's multiculturalism, but they've probably never heard of the word. They live it. It's a good thing that the up-and-coming, artsy-fartsy, nuevo, urban, pioneer, multicultural vultures think bingo is below them. Otherwise they might have invaded us and turned our evenings into performance art or a documentary film by an urban anthropologist. A social engineer might have come to study the leisure habits of inner-city inhabitants for an Urban Studies class.

Why are there no "Suburban Studies" classes at the university? Or how about "Owning-Class Culture and Customs 101," or "Ethics in Corporate Culture," or "How to Become a Bureaucrat"? I'm straying off the subject. Now, Julia, where were you? Ah, reclaiming my working-class roots now that I'm ascending the ladder of success, moving on up from welfare class to unemployed/underemployed working poor with no medical—borrowing money left and right, in some ways worse off than if we had stayed on the public tit.

Yes, roots reclaimed. No longer ashamed of my grandpa and uncles who worked themselves to death, or drank themselves to demise, or both. Instead of disgust, I marvel in the memory of dirty fingernails and rough-hewn calloused hands of working-class men, many with missing fingers and/or limbs and cut scars, phantoms of the factory or some war or a knife fight out of control. Hands bear the story lips won't tell. Maybe they just got disfigured with one of their machines in the toolshed, making something or fixing someone's broken whatever. Like you, Bob. You made your own house and garden decorations out of throwaways, bicycle parts, and tin cans—recycling before it was popular. It's known as "tacky." I love how you showed my boys how to become Ace #1 garbage pickers—furnished our house, decorated it, too.

Big generous heart, you working-class man, and smart too—not in the book-learned way, but sharp nonetheless. You can smell something stinking in Denmark real quick. You get to the point and see what's real, but I wonder if you ever knew just how smart you were. Working-class intelligence may not proffer them big 65-cent words. It's kind of, well, wordless at times—like the gut sense, the "I'll sleep on it" problem solving, and the "gotta move my body, work my hands" kind of thing. It's very physical and intuitive and connected to head thinking but not entirely in one's head. You can think on your feet, on your back, and in a jam. The way you show people how you care for them is intelligence, and it is as eloquent as any poem.

No human services, social services, service learning, or professional human beings here, just folks who share their gifts, talents, and skills—you know, doing for others and others doing for you, whatever is needed at the time. Given and taken freely. And to think that I almost missed out on appreciating all these wonderful things about being working class over a hurt called *ashamed*. Hmmmm. The more I think about stuff, the more I wonder what purpose it possibly serves to make people feel bad about who and what they are. Where did it come from, and who profits from it?

Is it really progress that we're cooped up in a computer terminal talking to one another on e-mail? I don't think so. I'd rather be out in my toolshed, or garden, in the mix, tending my new angel plants. I am grateful to you, Bob, and to Stan, Uncle Tom, Grandpa Bud, Harold, Chuck, Don, and all the working-class men who took time with me, who showed me who they are by being pleased with themselves and living their lives. I think I'll try to keep the traditions of the heart alive in my way and become a keeper of connections in the spirit of those who are gone now but have left a generous living legacy in my heart.

Roots reclaimed. Ah . . . that's so much better!

Introduction to "When We Left Minneapolis"

THIS LITTLE PIECE OF WRITING WAS MY FIRST ATTEMPT to fashion words into anything longer than a song or poem. My three sons and I had moved up to Isle, Minnesota, near Lake Mille Lacs during the time of increasing gang violence in our South Minneapolis neighborhood. The *New York Times* had characterized my hometown as *Murderapolis*. The sad commentary was proven by frequent requests for me to sing at funerals for youngsters and community members who fell victim to death by handgun. Raising children became all the more challenging in an environment where my sons had *bullet drills* on the playground. Holding one's breath for the next traumatic event to unfold was the daily exercise of autonomic response to stressors of this nature. I remember wondering out loud about programs that brought children from Northern Ireland for extended visits in our state so they could experience a measure of peace. I said, "They must not be staying in my neighborhood, and they sure didn't read the newspapers!"

Our family spent two years in Isle, out on a little lake. On the day of our arrival a lovely glow in pinstriped hues arched across the water. Rainbow's end appeared as if it were touching the ground's edge that was our new front yard. Yes, I did feel the promise of hope in new beginnings for my family. The boys said they felt like we were *Little House on the Prairie*—Dinsmore style. When deer hunting season arrived, we were very scared and slept on the living room floor all together. The sound of gunshots took our urban shell-shocked selves by surprise. I remember my son Jacob noticing that the gas station stores out in the country did not have bulletproof windows. It broke my heart to hear such observations. He was nine at the time.

Living fourteen miles out of town, we spent a lot of time in the van going to and from school and doctor visits. We noticed how people in the country never let the opportunity to greet one another pass them by. Motorists and pedestrians alike waved their hands in a generous and lively manner. It didn't take long for us to incorporate this little blessing into our daily life. For the first several months we were afraid to go outside, partly because of leftover city traumas, and then because our move coincided with hunting season. We lived on a lake, and the boys played video fishing games on electronic toys in the house. After a short time, they decided to take their video gear to the pawnshop and exchange Nintendos for fishing poles and tackle boxes. I so enjoyed watching my sons learn to fish out on the rickety little dock in front of the lake house. There was a view from the living room, kitchen, dining room, and porch. They were safe under my eye, under the big sky, under eagle's wings.

I finally exhaled. They did too!

When We Left Minneapolis

I feel like a refugee
from my beloved home,
my city,
my neighborhood,
the place where my mother was born,
and I, and my children, too.
I miss the busyness of my city,
the streets teeming with playing children
and the ever-droning sound of the freeway my grandfather fought.

A long time ago, my grandpa and his neighbors gathered themselves and their determination to fight the coming 35W. They met at St. Stephen's Catholic Church, some with their shotguns, to strategize their oppositions to the big motorway. They fought and lost.

The long concrete riverbed soon cut through vital communities, spewing its engine thunder, which some say sounded the death knell of the life we knew in the old neighborhood. Progress came speeding in on screeching rubber and grinding metal to disrupt the complex weave of relationships born of time, trust, care, conflict, and compassion that was the community I grew up in. At least my grandfather made a stand. He had the famous Irish spirit in him.

The Irish know about hard times. We survived brutal colonization by helping one another in family and community. Our slave labor paid passage out of times of starvation and famine that were exploited to destroy us.

We are singers of sad songs
and seed sowers of justice.
We are a proud and strong people,
known by our brawn that helped build cities
and feared for the rage that boils
just below the surface
of our warm, smiling eyes.
We are weavers of words
and masters of melody
and have a song for everything.
Everything.

I must have that same kind of spirit in me. My mother said that I was born with the lungs of an opera singer. I was the loudest crier in the nursery at St. Mary's Hospital. My face was black and blue from a hard birth, so I guess I came into this world fighting and feeling beaten up. I still cry very loudly. You could probably say I wail. In the olden days my people called it *keening*, and those who could weep and wail just so were highly respected and were called upon in times of grief for wakes and funerals and such. I imagine they helped others express sorrows and feelings of loss.

The music that I play is very heartfelt. I often am asked to sing at funerals, and many people cry when they hear me. I have loved singing since the very first time I sang. In fact, singing was my preferred language as a child. I never could quite grasp king's English and had troubles with reading, so I was quiet a lot because I felt like I was dumb. It seemed that only singing and music were a language full enough to contain the true parts of myself. I have always felt very connected to my passions and intelligence as they come up through my breath in song.

My first remembrance of hearing music was hearing my mother singing "TuRaLuRa" and "I'll Take You Home Again, Kathleen" and other songs relating to the Irish-American immigrant experience. She would sing loud at night, accompanying herself on the piano, waiting for my father to come home from his pub wanderings. I heard that my father could croon a heartrending "Danny Boy" at the piano bar, which was his home away from home. Lyrics of leaving and of being left filled my early musical memories. So this lamenting by way of song is in my Irish blood.

I learned about singing for joy, as well, but that was shown to me outside of my immediate family by the folks at the Gospel Temple Church in St. Paul. After attending service there with my cousin, who married into a big gospel-singing family, I could barely stay awake at Catholic Mass. Catholic music pre-Vatican II was rather dirgelike in comparison. I loved the Gregorian chants, but I never did learn Latin, so I didn't know what it was speaking to. It must have been about God this and church that. It was lovely in a way, but it didn't pull me in. At the Gospel Temple, people moved their bodies to the time and clapped their hands and sang loud and got happy, and some even danced when they felt the Spirit. And there were harmonies—glorious harmonies—and great emotion. Thelma Buckner and the Minnesota Gospel-Singing Twins, all three sets of whom were born from this amazing woman, could sing a person to heaven and back on the collective sound of their glory!

Somehow through the teachers and teachings of my beloved Catholic faith, I had picked up the notion that my body was bad and sinful. I will always be grateful to the people at the Gospel Temple for showing me the beauty and grace of the human body being alive in this way. I remember feeling very in love with life, as though I must have been born into the wrong culture or something, because I just wanted to stay there and sing, dance, and sing some more.

So here I am again, feeling out of place, out of time, in the wrong space. Here I am, lamenting with these words I am writing, marks on a paper—a new language I'm discovering. Maybe I write now because my sadness is so heavy it will break my voice if I try to sing it. Maybe the weight of my grief will crack my breath too hard and there will be no song. Maybe there's already too many songs sung about leaving anyway. So I'll make this writing instead.

I feel like a refugee
from my beloved home,
my city,
my neighborhood,
the place where my mother was born,
and I, and my children, too.

One day several months ago, right before spring break, I packed my kids some clothes and we left home. We just drove out of the city and didn't go back. Out here where the silence is very silent and the dark night extremely so (except when there is a moon), I hope to collect my thoughts and put them in a little book. I hope to heal from post–urban traumatic shock and assist my children in detoxifying from bad air, dirty water, and daily violence. I hope we can grieve all of the loving relationships that have stressed and strained under the weight of these unraveling times. I call it the Great Coming-Apart Times.

There certainly is more physical space out here for children to run and play, and sing out, and be who they are.

I'm lonesome and scared. I'm of the city; my kids are fifth-generation city. I love fast food, and how is a welfare single mother from the white trash urban nomad tribe who doesn't shave her legs supposed to survive out here anyway?

I'll just trust myself to do what I came here to do, and maybe I, too, will remember how to run and play, and sing out, and be who I am.

Note: Being greeted by a rainbow on the day we moved to the lake felt like heaven's welcome to a future with new possibilities. Sadly, though, it turned out to signal the beginning of endings and loss. It was the last time we were to live as a family.

Cold Day Thankfulness

Wind chill -60°, February 1, 1996, Isle, Minnesota

LORD, THANK YOU FOR MOVING THE DISTRACTIONS out of my world today via bitter cold incompatible with electricity. Thank you for stilling radio, TV, and telephone accoutrements of modern living, for now I can hear the sound of conversation with you.

Thank you for clearing the dark clouds that linger around the pain of jealousy, thieving, greed, and disrespect—in others and myself. I'm starting to glimpse more clearly who you really made me to be. Thank you. Thank you, because seeing in color is way more interesting and enjoyable than the shadow hues painted by doubt and fear. More and more I'm noticing goodness when it is happening—a canvas in rainbow—and vibrant indeed!

Thank you for delivering my children and me from the violence of too much poverty, the poverty of too much wealth, the destruction of guns and boardrooms, and most of all, the hurt of not knowing your love for so long. I'm learning how it feels to experience care and concern. Thank you for the holy balm of your grace and mercy.

Thank you for taking my kids and me from church basement feedings, government commodity food lines, and the food shelves that give out dead food, but thank you even for that. Thank you that I have now tasted alive and nourishing vegetables, grown by hands that tend the plant and soil with gentle respect. Thank you in advance for how you will make provision to afford organic more often.

Thank you for the memory of the smell of a rose, the air after lightning, and the pungent big earth in its soggy thaw. Thank you for the scent of fresh baby. But, Lord, please keep the heavy perfumes away.

Thank you for the spacious glories that greet me each dawn, as the sun, mist, and clouds slow waltz their way over the edge of the horizon in all manner of shades of blessing.

Thank you for this freezing day of stark stillness, just quiet enough to hear each note of this spirit music and heart song of giving thanks!

Angels Unaware?

MOLD IN THE LAKE HOUSE? Post urban traumatic stress? Perhaps arsenic found in the soil of our yard in South Minneapolis was to blame. God forbid that the increasingly difficult behaviors of my twins should have anything at all to do with the family curse of mental illness. I had managed to support us for two years but did not have medical coverage. I had to sell the van to qualify for the state assistance program, because it was $703 over the asset limit. You can't stay afloat in the country without dependable transportation. Special needs day care did not exist, and I got sick with multiple chemical sensitivities. Doctor appointments, hospitalizations, school Individual Education Planning meetings, and inadequate children's mental health services interfered with my ability to earn income. Our options? Either to give up custody of my son to the county, where he'd go into long-term foster care, or move. The goodbyes were hard. We had finally settled in to our new community. Isaac and Jacob hadn't tried to ride their bicycles back to Minneapolis (one hundred miles) for nearly eighteen months. The high school students in study halls where I worked were sad to see us go. All I wanted to do was work and raise the boys, but doing so became more difficult with each passing month.

We moved to a mid-sized town close to a hospital and better family support infrastructures, or so I thought. The shelter was an old Catholic convent. They allowed us to move in with our extended family, which included a dog, two birds, and sixteen hamsters. Starting all over is hard work, especially when you've lost every gain made along the way. Eventually I found a house to rent. I remember reading *Angela's Ashes,* (one of the up to ten books of my entire reading career) on the couch, which was a mattress on the floor of the living room that doubled as my bedroom. One day it was bitter cold and the furnace malfunctioned. By the time my boys returned from school, the birds and hamsters were dead from carbon monoxide poisoning. Then the pipes burst. Ceilings rained down upon our heads in wet chunks of plaster and paint chips. The nice landlords dropped an industrial fan off for drying the carpet on their way to vacation in the Bahamas. Frankie McCourt and his dear mother, Angela, were good company at that time. Things could, after all, be worse.

My eldest son made friends with several boys who enjoyed spending time fishing on the river nearly every day that following spring. I got a job as a waitress at a fancy restaurant, and the twins were attending a school with good special education programming. We began to settle into another new community. I met Jerome at my new job as he trained me in the particulars of food serving. He was quite the character and good company. We started dating and eventually became engaged. That man loved getting an education. When we met he was working on two graduate degrees, and some months later even attended two different universities at the same time! Jerome enjoyed getting married and having babies as much as he enjoyed getting college degrees, one of the reasons I never married him. That he was a PK (preacher's kid) wasn't a surprise. PKs and I go all the way back to my childhood. Everything I ever learned about sex, drugs, and rock 'n' roll was from offspring of the ordained ministerial kind. His opinions were many and loud in decibel. In short order I came to learn of certain circumstances hanging over the head of Jerome, which caused concern for the people who cared about me.

Apparently, selling cocaine had been one of his creative methods for financing his education. He'd been caught up in a sting some time before we met and was in the legal process of refusing to be turned. He, being the little fish with aspirations that included living in the free world, had been the target of opportunity by law enforcement in an undercover setup. Jerome never rolled on the big fish, and he eventually went to prison for seven years, which was another reason we didn't get married. Family and friends had opinions, some of which were shared out loud, regarding my relationship with this man of colorful inclinations. At the time, I was so very tired. Really, I could have lain down and gone to sleep forever on many of those days. Jerome was wonderful company. He was full of life and didn't want to miss one precious minute of freedom while staring down the barrel of a long incarceration. It was he who taught me scripture about *the power of life and death being in the tongue*, and *greater is he who is in me than he who is in the world.* Jerome was a fallen-away minister. He let his license to preach expire by choice, as he told it, because of knowing three preachers who were struck dead in a row. According to his interpretation of events unexplainable, hypocrisy's recompense was to blame for their untimely deaths. He was really good with the boys, instructing on the errors of his own example in life choices, helping with homework, and cheering up their depressed mother.

Before getting locked up, Jerome became obsessed with the idea that my eldest son should be enrolled into a program called Upward Bound, housed at the local state university. He said this college prep experience had saved his own life while growing up on the mean streets of Chicago's South Side. Daniel, at the time, was one year too young for consideration, and the program had just met capacity in its enrollment anyway, so I was perplexed by Jerome's insistence that we keep trying for a spot. His gifts did include vocal skills in persuasion. I told him he should go to law school, where his pontifications might be more appreciated, as my plate was already overfilled. Servicing the social services that had crept back into the realms of my family was a time-consuming affair. Persistence being Jerome's middle name, it turned out that Danny was accepted into the program. During the slow melt of spring, he moved onto the college campus. Warm breezes shed excess of winter's accumulated snowstorm, resulting in a season of unprecedented flooding along Minnesota's rivers. The week my son started Upward Bound, two young men in the program went fishing on a sunny day. They were washed away in the powerful current of water's sparkling, deceptive lure.

We lasted nine months in that town. Circumstances in obtaining that which might meet basic needs for my children and I became quicksand of our descent into hell. Vague feelings welled up in my being at so many turns that met with disastrous consequences. Senses of snakes in the grass, unseen but still stinging, were feelings of being run out of town. Years later I was to uncover a letter sent to that county department of social services warning them of our arrival. In it, it was said that I had the nerve to call Senator Wellstone for assistance because I disagreed with practices that force parents to give up custody of their children in order to obtain medical care. I learned to trust my instincts after finding that document, but not until after moving to yet another town, a town where we would try to start over. This town had an adolescent psychiatric wing where my son would not have to be strapped to a bed with football players hired to guard against his escape. Perhaps I would not be told to give up custody of two children who were in crisis by that time. I don't think Daniel ever forgave me for the timing of that move. It was in the middle of football season in the year that his high school team made it all the way to the state playoffs without him.

Knowing Jerome was the bright spot of my experiences lived in the town upon the river. I also believe he was an angel unaware. Looking at the circumstances in his life could have prompted me to stay away from the drug dealer, baby daddy frequent, and collector of ex-wives and college degrees. I appreciated his energy, intelligence, and enthusiasm. His infectious pizzazz refreshed my grip that was holding my family together. Besides, God had shown me a glimpse of how Jerome was going to be used down the road for purposes in the Almighty's divinely unfolding plans. With that big mouth, sharp mind, and caring heart, articulating experiences in and of the prison industrial complex, he would surely come in handy to God. He does not stop caring for people just because they are behind bars. Society may lack compassion for those people who are labeled criminal, but God? No way!

So, it came as no surprise to me when Jerome, some ten years later, conducted a workshop at a sociology conference. His subject? Prison recidivism. In-depth interviews with fellow inmates were on videos he planned to show. The occasion was particularly momentous because his presentation included coming out of the closet marked *convicted felon* to his colleagues. I felt proud of how he met life's challenges, and told him so. There had never been a doubt in my mind that this day would come. Now he is Dr. Jerome. He teaches at the university where my son's life might very well have been saved. He's married and is the father of several more children. Jerome was the angel unaware to my family and perhaps to others as well. I have forgiven him for all the times he said that I would be a dangerous woman if I had any class. The class I have is quite all right with me. It helps me to see truth and beauty unfolding in the messiness of our soul's refinement. It helped me to see him pretty clearly!

As for the answer to his question, "How are the children?" They are all alive!

I wrote a song for him and mailed it to the prison when he started his sentence.

Song for Jerome

You came into my world,
A life on shaky ground.
Ready to give up,
Hope was nowhere to be found.
My heart was closed and shriveled,
Protection from my hurts.
You came along and loved me up,
And broke a family curse.
You see, from my earthbound father
No love did I receive.
So a Father in the heavenlies,
A concept I could not perceive.
The tender care you showed me
Was enough to pull me through
The depths of desperation
To a life that's been renewed.
Our Father up in heaven,
Hallowed be Thy name.
His love He gave through you to me.
I'll never be the same.
So let this be a lesson—
There are angels in our midst.
God uses the unlikely ones
To mill His holy grist.
Now as I live my life and wonder
What it is that I must do,
He gently whispers in my ear
To be the Christ to you.
Through Him, in Him, with Him,

We are ALL that we can be.
And by the Holy Spirit
He truly sets us free
From sin and condemnation
From coulds, and shoulds, and woulds,
For what the enemy wants for bad
God will work for good.
So, trust in Him with all your heart.
Be peaceful, Mr. J.
The Almighty has already
Delivered you from your games.
He knows your heart, and I do too,
So pure, so strong, and true.
He will guide you and direct you
To do what you must do.
I thank you and I bless you
As I move from day to day.
The gifts you gave and shared with me
Have blessed me on my way.
When you feel discouraged
And don't know where to turn,
Remember how God's loving words
Will help you to discern
Which path to take and where to go.
He's a lamp unto thy feet.
He's with us always everywhere—
In the prison . . .
In the street . . .
Harden not your heart, my love,
Though trials may annoy.
The enemy can never
Take away your joy.
And when the troubles seem too much
Just lift your heart and sing,
Thanking Him for your struggles.
Praise Him every day.

For in our darkest hour
And the stormiest of times,
He rains His fire down in us
Our spirit to refine.
He's seeking to accomplish
His works in you and me,
So we can know His loving peace
And truly be set free.
My prayer for you today, my friend,
Is that you will always know
That I do love and care for you
Enough to let you go.
I will surely miss you,
More than you will ever know.
But holding something that's not yours
Doesn't help you grow.
So fare thee well—I thank you.
You are precious to my heart.
I never will forget you
Even though we're far apart.
My love for you is always,
Forever and a day.
And should we meet again, my friend,
I'll look in your eyes and say –
My heart was closed and shriveled,
Protection from my hurts.
You came along and loved me up
And broke a family curse!

Always, Rose

*"Every branch in Me that does not bear fruit He takes away; and every branch
that bears fruit He prunes, that it will bear more fruit. . . . I am the vine, you
are the branches. He who abides in me, and I in him, bears much fruit; for
without Me you can do nothing."*—John 15:2, 5

Part C. Terrible Storms, Night's Weeping Endured

Be Careful What You Pray For

Thankful to John and Cindy Gudhal, and Mother Sharon Witherspoon who threw down mightily.

THE YEAR WAS 1997. MY TWELVE-YEAR-OLD SON was on a collision course with death. I knew it, his twin brother knew it, and in the way my mother knows things, she did as well. A few months before the tragedy, a phone call came to my home from the office of Senator Paul Wellstone. His staffer, a woman I'd known from attending Mass at the Catholic Church of St. Stephan, was on the line asking me if everything was all right with the boys. Apparently, Mother had called with a frantic story about a social worker putting the life of my son Isaac in grave danger. She feared his death might be imminent! "Oh, that would be my mother; she's a bit out there these days," I explained, adding that it had been quite the challenge to get appropriate medical care for my sons. "Yes, we moved again. Perhaps things will get better here in Duluth. I had to leave Isaac behind just until Jacob is stabilized and we settle into the new surroundings." Our conversation ended with discussion of a charter school I was helping get off the ground that held hope for my twins to attend successfully. The public school district didn't always meet the educational needs of the class of children they belonged to, and I was not up for yet another battlefield, already too plentiful in the territory of being a Dinsmore.

Truth is, I had been worn nearly to a nub by several years of fruitless efforts to access needed community supports that allow children experiencing brain and biochemistry disorders to remain in their families. Help for my family either didn't exist or was always out of reach, and it seemed that not even an act of Congress could be useful to our situation. Seeing no cure for mental illness on the horizon, and having learned the hard way that medical coverage lacked in parity when it came to care and treatment, I was at a loss for what to do next.

When does a mother stop trying to get help for her child? Adversarial relationships with social service systems that are strapped for resources are a common experience for parents like me. Another lesson of the hard kind came from the experience of pushing up against county governmental systems that depend on economic incentives gained from assuming custody of our children. This breaking of families can be a particular kind of hell. Had I known how my children would suffer under systemic abuse, I would have let them take their chances on the streets. Retribution was a cruel hand from expectations that public servants at least meet legally mandated minimum standards of practice. Yes, even at their young age, had I known what was in store for us, I never would have tried to get help for them.

I found solace, comfort, and strength to live the not-so-easy life that was mine, in the company of elders at an African Methodist Evangelical church in our neighborhood. If the world had no cure for brain disorders, perhaps the miracles needed by my family might be possible through prayer and fasting. I beseeched God to break any generational curse contained in genetic material that might be the cause of illness or disorder in my children. Availing myself of instructions in righteous living and spiritual growth became activities of my earnest intentions. I began learning lessons in forgiveness and how its practice applied to my well-being. I learned that harboring unforgiveness blocked blessings and was stuff that is unbecoming in a person. To put it plainly, I began to see that unforgiveness looks ugly in people. It does not go with our shoes. I wished to cast off burdens caused by the linger of resentments and old hurts. Rolling over to get out of bed in the morning felt like performing a feat of Olympic strength. Yes, this aptly describes my condition when I decided to make a fearless and searching inventory to determine the source of the extra weight that was too much for me to carry any longer.

I constructed a list of people and occasions connected to memories of feeling wounded and wronged. Writing the name of the first person that popped into my mind for whom I felt an attachment of unresolved emotional pain gave way to the next, and the next person after that. This recollection was done gingerly and at a speed sufficient for acknowledging the nature of each relationship and its associated hurt. When this exercise was finished, I experienced a tangible measure of relief. My perception of the air about my aura sensed atmosphere less dense. Fleeting tinges of cleanly scrubbed ethers wafted throughout my apartment like the smell outside after lightning. Offenses built up over the course of a lifetime deserve to be untangled with time, attention, and loving care. It is the work done in process. *Father God,* began my prayer. *Thank you for sending a living example of forgiveness to walk around with us. Please help me to unpack my burdens in a good way. They're too heavy. Please help me to forgive all the people on my list. Help me to be bigger than my hurts. Father God, thank you for looking after my children. Amen.* I went to bed secure in the knowledge that a first step had been taken on the journey that is forgiveness.

Around 4:00 A.M. I awoke from the depths of peaceful sleep with a startle and a compelling physical sensation just below my belly button that felt like something stirring around and around. I don't know why, but I immediately dialed the number to the youth shelter that my son Isaac's social worker had placed him in.

When a male voice answered, words couldn't fly out of my mouth quickly enough. *"Where is my son? I am Isaac Dinsmore's mother, and I need to know if he is . . ."*

The man on the other end cut me off. He sounded nervous as he asked why I was calling, and if the state patrol had contacted me, and that someone should have called me by now.

"What is going on with my son? Put him on the line. I need to talk to him right now." As my insistence pressed through distance, the strange stirring in my belly continued.

"Is Isaac hurt? Why won't you tell me what is going on?" The man's voice, in tone serious, tone laden by dread's load, tone unforgettable to my ear, cut through the verbal barrage of my pleading to say, "Your son has been a fatality in a car wreck. Someone from the state patrol was supposed to call you. The last I heard was that he was en route to the nearest trauma center. I think it was HCMC, but they couldn't save your son and . . ."

I didn't hear anything more after that and hung up on him. The next call was to the Hennepin County Medical Center (HCMC) some hundred and more miles south. "I'm looking for my son. He's twelve years old. His name is Isaac Dinsmore. He was in a car wreck. Is he there?"

Someone came on the line and told me that Isaac's next of kin should come immediately and that we should prepare for the worst. I remember blurting out that my car was broken down, to which the person on the other end suggested I get on a medical emergency flight out of the Duluth airport. I hung up on that person as well.

Then I called a woman I had met only the day before. Her phone number was on a piece of paper lying in my sight. I asked her to drive me and Isaac's brothers to Minneapolis, as there had been an accident. While hasty preparations for getting on the road were made, I called several elders and others whom I had known to be prayer warriors of the knee-bone praying kind and asked for their intercession on behalf of my son who was only twelve and, therefore, too young to die. The swirling sensation continued stirring and turning in my belly. Family members residing near the hospital were contacted as well.

Daniel, Jacob, myself, our springer spaniel Lucy, and the dear woman whose little blue compact carried the tight squeeze of us down 35W, must have been quite a sight when we rolled through the doors at HCMC in various states of dress and undress, dog barking and all. There to meet us was the chaplain who put his arm around my shoulders while offering the standard greeting for bereaved persons, "I'm so sorry to . . ."

His sympathy was interrupted by a rather demanding tenor of female voice in the shrill of near hysteria, *"I'll be hearing nothing of that sort of talk, sir. Now take me to my son. He's going to be just fine, and I won't hear anything to the contrary. Where is he?"* I heard the sound of my voice as if it were coming over the hospital's speaker system. That must have been an out-of-body experience. Then I heard someone say, *"She's in denial."*

Walking down the corridor and around a corner was an auntie. She, having been in recovery from a divorce, had recently taken classes in the grief process. I remember brushing right past her extended hand like a barrel rolling down a hill. Proceeding around another corner and through a doorway, we arrived in a space that must have been a family waiting room. It was full of people I recognized as my relations, but a semitransparent haze of thickness in the air hung like a static cloud of smoke. *This is just great—now I'm hallucinating,* was a thought among racing thoughts and sensations, the chemistry of panic in full throttle.

In the moments it took to look upon each of the strained eyes there looking back at me, the sensation that we had only parted company a few hours ago did not jive with reality. There were years lying between then and when we were last in one another's company. Again, I scanned faces in the room, slowly, deliberating them one by one. *Oh my!* I realized that every person named on the previous evening was present, those for whom I bore unforgiveness. Yes, all were there save one.

"Everyone in our family is here except Mom," was my observation out loud.

Someone said we shouldn't let her know what happened because it would probably tip her off the edge of reality. The statement met with a chorus of murmuring agreements that it was in her best interest not to know about the accident.

Someone else chimed in, *"Yeah, she's been one can short of a six pack lately."*

Not even sixty seconds passed when my sister's cell phone rang. It was the sheriff's office calling to say that they had my mother down at the HCMC hospital and were admitting her to the intensive care psychiatric unit, and could someone please come to assist with her admission paperwork. *"Well, looks like Ma made it here after all,"* was my next observation. It seems I'm always stating the obvious.

Waiting for the doctor who was supposed to come tell me the status of my son took too long. Before you could spit on a stick, I was stating the obvious again, only these utterances were sentiments laced with pain.

"I don't know what you all came here for. Where were you when it was his birthday, or Christmas, or when he needed an extended family? Don't you think it's a bit late to finally show up now that he's on his deathbed?" Thank God my dear friend Minister Sarah Shannon arrived when she did. I was hot and hard to handle. My tongue needed taming, and she was just the person to handle that job. There is much more in the telling of this story, but its time has not arrived yet. I will, however, share a few poignant details with readers.

On the ride down 35W, at approximately three-quarters of the distance of our journey, Isaac's twin brother and I both experienced a deep peace. I can only describe it as I have heard others do, that it was a peace that passes all understanding. At the very same moment we both remarked out loud, in voice lifted not by our own power of decision but by assurance blessed into existence by a power greater than our own, *"Isaac will live."* During the time of feeling this great comfort the strange stirring in my belly stopped.

Apparently, Isaac and two girls snuck out of the youth shelter window after everyone else was asleep. A trucking company located near the shelter was easy access to cars with keys left inside. One of the girls had taken a car from that location two weeks prior. Somewhere between Willmar and Savage, a high-speed police chase had occurred. The officer suspected a drunk driver was behind the wheel. It was a thirteen-year-old girl trying to outrun the squad car when at 95 mph she lost control and the vehicle flipped end over end. Isaac, in the passenger seat, was propelled out onto the ground, where the car crushed his head. The two girls were pinned to their seats by the force of centrifuge and miraculously suffered only minor bumps and bruises. Isaac, however, had been listed as a fatality over the state patrol Teletype.

When Isaac could finally speak again, he told me that people's prayers were visible as streaming lights. He saw this and other things. He said it was hard to lay back down into his body, because he had to take the excruciating pain. I need to respect issues of his privacy with what he reported, so I will share just one more thing he told me. He said he was trying to come home for Mother's Day, but when he was hovering over his body, he thought I didn't want him anymore and he was not sure if he really wanted to live.

I slept in a little room just around the corner from the pediatric intensive care traumatic brain injury unit for weeks. There was a glowing sphere of light hovering there for the entire duration of my stay. It measured about the same circumference as a basketball. I don't know exactly what it was, but its emanation bathed the room and me with peace and comfort. It was the color very bright white.

My mother's hospitalization just happened to coincide with the length of weeks that numbered Isaac's initial recovery period. The psychiatric unit was handily located just above the pediatric floor. Her company and humor the finely-tuned frequency that was medicine in laughter. She, being prone to certain unexplainable interactions with properties of electricity, did not report any unusual energy happenings during this stay, but her wit (like Erma Bombeck on LSD) was in rare form. The circumstances called for a balm peculiar. Stories about the magical powers of new immigrant neighbors in her high rise had me doubled over with hilarity. Details recounted how men's thoughts transformed into fingers that unbuttoned, unzipped, and untied her clothing at the congregant dining hall every mealtime. The police refused to arrest them for indecent contents of mind, and neither the governor nor President Clinton would return her phone calls. Visits with Mother brought blessed relief from the serious business just downstairs and made those weeks bearable!

I don't know if Isaac has ever understood the complications that became my acquiescence to agree with a voluntary transfer of custody. I was promised this would assure the care he was in need of. I will go to my grave regretting that day. I'm sure he knows I love him, and that I have always wanted him and his twin brother as well.

While he was still in intensive care, the social service agency responsible for misplacing him into the youth shelter made plans to terminate my parental rights and started the process of assembling an attractive adoption package. That was the cue that a CYA was under way. (That's cover your ass where I'm from.) No one in their right mind would try to put a twelve-year-old boy up for adoption with absolutely no history of family abuse or neglect. I had to fight this off with no help from anyone. I waited a long time for the social worker and her supervisor to apologize. They never did.

I found a lawyer to take up a case to hold the county accountable, so that no other family might have to endure the kind of systemic abuse mine did. He wanted to go for the deep pockets of the trucking company. I wanted him to go for jumping the legal immunity with impunity our public servants have been granted by guess who? You and I. With no way to hold our public agencies accountable, they can and do get away with harming the very people they're charged with serving and protecting. The case was on its way to our state supreme court when more tragedy came to our door. The case was dropped.

It was pretty dumb of me to take on a system that had unlimited power and money. I had no social support, no legal defense fund, and the retribution that came upon my children was unspeakable. So we suffered. We continue to suffer. Sometimes I have trouble getting out of bed. I tell college students my story in hopes that they will go into these systems and transform them and change the immunity laws. The youngsters give me hope.

A couple of things learned from this experience: You should be very careful about biting the hand that feeds you. Also, after walking into the HCMC family room to see everyone on the list I had made only the night before . . . Well, I'd say to be careful what you pray for! I have a new list of unforgiveness to unburden myself of now. Isn't it always something? Lord, help us all!

Don't Give Up

For my beloveds, Pat and Connie

Chorus:
When the dark seems the darkest,
And part of you feels like dying,
Just remember you're not alone,
And you're always welcome
. . . To come home.

Verse 1
There's enough for me,
And there's plenty for you.
Let us sit at the table
And drink to the truth
That each of us is precious,
We're loved beyond compare,
And I like the way we break down walls
With the simple words "I care."

Verse 2
There's enough love in this room
To fill the deepest ocean.
It's a power to behold
That stirs me with emotion.
It's really quite amazing,
As I take a look around,
To see the caring and commitment
To the ties that bind abound.

Verse 3
In our days we live and struggle
To take one at a time.
Don't fret about the future,
Leave past mistakes behind.
Be now consumed by loving's will,

Hold on strong and be held tight,
Drink a cup of sweet forgiveness,
Claim your birthright.

Verse 4
Be no longer sorrow's victim.
There's no reason now to fight.
It's possible to choose each day
To walk within the light.
Give yourself completely—body, mind, and soul—
To those who love and cherish you,
and all the ones who know . . . that you can't . . .

Depth Charges

Judge Not, and you shall not be judged. Condemn not, and you shall not be condemned. Forgive and you will be forgiven."—Luke 6:35, 37

Bootstraps!

I'm neither a Republican nor a Democrat. When it comes to public policy with regard to economic opportunity and the poor, the view from my window has looked like this: Republicans have expected us to pick ourselves up by nonexistent bootstraps, and Democrats make the bootstraps so darned complicated they're useless.

Stigma

When is the last time you heard about a spaghetti dinner, quilt raffle, or other type of community fund-raiser to help pay for the catastrophic medical bills associated with a family struggling with a member with mental illness?

Did You Hear?

Did you hear about the interviews with Fortune 500 executives that took place in the days and hours near the end of their lives? When asked if there was anything they would go back and do differently, *they all* said they'd spend more time with children and family and share a greater measure of their wealth!

Short Survey

In the last decade, city planning efforts to deconcentrate urban poverty have resulted in the relocation of the poor to suburban communities of Minneapolis and St. Paul, where there are very few sidewalks. Increasing numbers of low-wage earners and people on fixed incomes cannot afford to own automobiles. Lengthy walking distances to a bus stop are often the case. Which of the following do you think might effect the quickest route to the creation of safe pedestrian zones?

(A) An outcry from local homeowners on behalf of their new neighbors, due to obvious safety issues after a child is killed trying to cross a busy stretch of roadway. In addition to the absence of sidewalks, there was no stoplight on the child's three-mile route to school, where he wanted to participate in extracurricular sports activities (happened this year near my home).

(B) Local homeowners campaign for *greenway* leisure and fitness walking paths.

(C) In their spare time, walking residents organize an effort to plan, rezone, and appropriate sparse dollars for pedestrian traffic.

(D) Sidewalk issues become obsolete when the low-wealth residents are displaced. The cheaply constructed, privately owned apartment complexes are full of mold, and there's more money to be made by converting property into condo developments that current renters cannot afford.

ANSWER: Your guess is as good as mine!

A Question Redirected (If I May Bend Your Ear for a Moment)

To the people whose deeply concerned question is, Why do so many poor people feel entitled to food stamps, medical care, and other forms of welfare? Besides the fact that our government named them entitlement programs, my first response is another question: Why are you not as concerned about the very few who control the bulk of resources and wealth in our country? and Why it is they feel entitled to hoard it?

I also recommend reading up on the spiritual disease psychotherapist Jessie O'Neill has identified as *affluenza:* a dysfunctional relationship with money/wealth or the pursuit of it. Globally it is a back up in the flow of money resulting in a polarization of the classes and a loss of economic and emotional balance.

I think an example of affluenza's pervasive reach is evident in the overarching reason American voters give for their reluctance to consider flat tax initiatives or other reforms that might increase tax rates of the wealthy. One of the symptoms of affluenza is a sense of false entitlement. We have all internalized entitlement beliefs to varied degrees that are entrenched deep within the psyche of our national mythology like a sacred shrine. Greed built the cathedral for a few, with the blood, sweat, and tears of many. Greed is ingenious and has fortified its hallowed cathedral walls by convincing the working masses to bow down to its thievery. We worship the birthright of every American to work, invest, or speculate our way into millionairedom. We uphold the right to have way more than a person needs. And we *sure* don't want to pay taxes on all that future largesse our brainwashed desire is fixated on. In my way of thinking, it seems as if we have traded in the planetary health and well-being of countless millions of people for the pipe dreams and counterfeit hope of amassing fictitious treasure chest fortunes!

I think Ms. O'Neil is so very smart to diagnose this spiritual ailment. I respect her for her courage and for recognizing that affluenza is not just a rich person's illness. Check her out at The Affluenza Project!

Many years ago I thought about designing a twelve-step national recovery program called Americans Anonymous, but now I would amend my program to Affluenza Anonymous.

Step 1. We all could admit to being powerless over manifest destiny thinking, false entitlement, and the consumption of too much of the world's resources.

Step 2. We all could come to believe that a power greater than ourselves could restore us to sanity, which would do wonders for our overinflated ethno/egocentrism.

Step 3. We all would turn our will and lives over to God, as we understand God and turn our extra wealth over to people, cultures, and natural realms on the planet that are facing extinction.

Battle Hymn for the Republic of Them That's Got

I got.
You won't.
I deserve.
You don't.
I need more.
You get less.
I have choice.
You stress.
Them that's got keep on getting.
So the song is sung.
I worked hard to get here.
And I want to have my fun.
I keep you out of sight and mind,
Your tales of woe too much a chore.
If I decide to help you just one time,
You'll keep on coming back for more.
I know ease and leisure.
You work and toil.
I eat best and better.
You eat food that spoiled.
I am the master.
You are the slave.
I name roads and buildings.
You can name your grave.
Them that's got keep on getting.
Them that's not shall surely lose.
It's not my fault where you were born.
Or that you can't afford some shoes.
Leave me alone. Don't bother mine.
There's nothing I can do.
My taxes have been paid
To care for the likes of you.
I got.
You don't.
Yes, that's what I said.

Your choices and bad karma
Is how you made your bed.
I deserve.
You don't.
It's my reward for who I am.
Too bad you didn't get your own
Or make a better plan.

Question and Answer

Recently a pastor asked, *"Julia, how is it that you can still smile as you do after suffering through so much hardship?"* I told him it is probably because of all the times I actually answered people's question—*"How are you?"*

When they asked, I told them, and then they ended up helping me bear the weight of burdens. It also caused more than a few people never to ask that again.

You see, the common greeting of *"Hello. How are you?"* is a loaded question for many.

Consider this: The American Psychological Association conducted a study on life stressors, the big ones—losing a job, moving, loss of health, death, etc. They were able to determine that average middle-class Americans can experience major life disruptions if one to three stressors occur over a short time period. The same study went on to say that poor people, regardless of race, are experiencing on any given day from six to eight stressors, often with little or no interruption between onsets.

Wow!

That might explain feeling so tired for much of my life!

Consider yourself warned.

The next time you see me and ask how I am or how things are going, I may tell you all about it, and then you can start feeling tired too. Or perhaps I might decide that your question is an opportunity to declare victory over my circumstances by answering with *"I'm too blessed to be stressed"* or *"Very well, thank you, and yourself?"* or *"Blessed and highly favored,"* or as Grandpa would say, *"Cookin' with gas!"* When you hear these statements, you can assume I am going through the worst part of a difficulty. At any rate, I would like to take this space to thank every person who has ever asked me, *"How are you?"* to whom I answered honestly, and upon our next encounter had the nerve to inquire again. Thank you! P.S. I am smiling just now.

Speaking of Smiles

If you ever talk to people up close and they back away, or if friends start offering you chewing gum or mints, get yourself to a dentist! It could be that you have bad breath, which can be a symptom of gum disease. I had not been to a dentist in over twenty-two years, which was fine with me. People messing with my mouth is something I'd rather avoid. Their big hands reaching too near my airway makes me feel like I'll suffocate! During the times when the kids and I did have Minnesota medical assistance, finding a dentist who would accept our insurance was next to impossible anyway.

When John Kerry ran for president, Cloquet, Minnesota, was the first stop on his hometown USA tour. I had been asked to play my guitar and sing with a bluegrass ensemble and then lead the crowd of six to eight thousand people in a patriotic song. With national media all around, the thought of my teeth flashing on the evening news had me trying to sing with a mouth partially closed, which is a dumb idea.

The Kerry gig reawakened my desire for a smile full of orderly, aligned pearly whites. To the good fortune of my mouth, I was able to locate a dentist who had an opening in his quota of medical assistance patients. I asked for a ballpark estimate in the cost to close gaps, put caps on, and any other procedure needed to make my teeth *pretty.* Knowing the price would be a first step toward making this dream a reality, I could start a teeth savings account or something. After the exam and X rays, I was told that my gum disease had progressed. My question was, *"What is the treatment?"* Dr. T.'s warm, compassionate chairside manner had my eyes full to brimming with salty water upon his answer.

"Your medical coverage will pay to remove all these teeth and fit you with dentures but will not reimburse for the deep gum cleaning you'd need to keep them."

With holy water flowing like a faucet, my rambling questions mumbled out between little quaking sobs. *"How much would it cost to save my teeth? I'm a singer and a performer. . . . My work is on the stage . . . in front of lots of people. . . . I make my living with my mouth. . . . What if the dentures fell out on a big long note? It has long been my dream to have nice looking teeth. . . . What can I do to keep them?"*

My raw, determined pleadings must have moved Dr. T., because the next thing I knew, a woman dental hygienist came into our little room and started poking, prying, and wiggling every tooth in my head. She said that a series of deep-to-the-root scraping sessions would be required to stop my gum disease . . . and told me how much it would cost. I'm quite sure the quote was at a huge discount. She may even have volunteered her labor, as the price was far too low to pay for six to eight sessions. (But the cost was still far out of my reach). Somehow our conversation revealed our common acquaintance with a certain Bill W. and my sons' mental health case manager. A brain flash of many long county car rides to various hospitals around the state with this social worker sped to the ledge of my lips, where verbal *ah ha's* tumbled out.

"Oh, yiii! That's why she always offered me breath mints before I even got my seat belt on. Ya know, I would talk her ear off for hundreds of miles. Your poor friend. She could have put politeness aside and just told me that my breath was terrible. No wonder I was allowed to smoke in the car—cigarette smell was probably easier to deal with. I never connected her breath mints and my mouth till now, which speaks to how much stress was sitting on me. Tell her I'm sorry; I'm tryin' to get it fixed, and if we ever have to ride together again, I'll bring my own mints. . . . okay?"

A rare and wonderful spirit filled that dental practice. Everyone from the receptionist to the doctors and technicians emanated light through their eyes and around their beings. Who would have thought I'd bump into Christ so many times in one day, and at the dreaded dentist of all places! Christ showed up again later that week via e-mail and a pair of eighty-plus-year-old twins who have acted like guardian angels toward me over time. Their electronic love spoke these words: *"Send name and address of dentist office . . . will mail check to help pay for dental care . . . want you to keep your teeth!!!"*

God is so good! I got all the gum scraping one could imagine and never suffocated even once. With diligent and correct flossing routines, my roots should hold for some time to come. The only problem with regard to my teeth and the stage is remembering not to eat just before a performance. Wee bits of leftover meals get stuck in all the new nooks and crannies from the deep cleaning, and did fly out of my singing mouth a couple of times. I think a few people noticed, but I can imagine feeling much more embarrassment if a denture plate took flight instead of food particulates! I'm very thankful to have my own teeth. Are you wondering why I didn't mention the dentist or clinic by name? They told me it was illegal to work with me in this way and that they could get into some kind of trouble with the so-and-so board and/or the such-and-such regulatory agency. Can you believe it? *I bless the names of Dr. T. and Hygienist M. at the L. Dental Clinic!*

Something Worth Writing About

I have received many accolades for leadership and community service. The prize I am most proud of was being honored as the Fan of the Year twice in a row at the Duluth Central high school football team's annual award banquet. The youngsters even created a new category of mention just for me!

Something Regrettable

I bumped into Sheila Wellstone when we were both asked to speak at a press conference for an affordable housing construction sight for single mothers. Throwing her arms around me with a warm hug, she asked me where in the world I had disappeared to for the last several years, making mention that she thought of me often. My reply was that the boys and I had slipped into seemingly unending depths of children's mental health hells. She then asked for me to elaborate. I wanted to revel in the joy of our short time together and said to schedule a long lunch with Paul and her, for just after the election when I would tell them both all about it. I so looked forward to our gathering, but just a few short weeks later they were both taken from us in the plane crash. Losing the unmatchable heart and soul of public leadership embodied in the Wellstones is grief still fresh some seven years later. I pray that mental health legislation just introduced in their name and honor will be passed into law. I hope the legacy and spirit of Paul and Sheila's compassion for Those People suffering under burdens of biobrain disorders, chemical addictions, and stigma will continue.

Home

One thing you lack: Go your way, sell whatever you have and give to the poor, and you will have treasure in heaven; and come, take up the cross, and follow me. —Mark 10:21

SPENDING TIME WITH AUNTIE SHEILA during the years I was a VISTA worker in the Phillips neighborhood afforded opportunities to hear stories of my family history. She would often remark, *"Julia, I swear, the government sprayed our neighborhood with some kind of chemical that made us all go crazy!"* She would say this over and again in different ways. Upon hearing this, people probably thought Auntie was touched in the head, and at times I might have agreed with them, except that time usually revealed the truths in what she'd said. Auntie had been born on All Saint's Day—Halloween—and someone said with a caul over her head. I've heard that babies birthed with a membrane covering their scalp and face have abilities in the second sight, the sixth sense, and ways of knowing the future. Being endowed with gifts in the realms of the mystical is nothing new to the Irish, but I think some family members are afraid of those of us who are sensitive in these ways, because it can look too much like mental illness.

Auntie told me about a springtime in the early '50s when several women in the neighborhood miscarried their babies. They would saunter down the block to visit with Grandma on the front porch and ask to hold my uncle who was a baby born healthy. I imagine this helped ease their sadness while moving through the process of grieving. Shortly thereafter, the government set up some kind of a free medical clinic nearby. Grandpa was suspicious about the government offering *anything* for free and said he did not trust their motives. Auntie remembers having to walk through some kind of a metal detector at the Clinton grade school in the mornings.

God Bless Paul Wellstone. He was the one who managed to get classified government files opened, for a minute, which proved the truth in Auntie's tellings. The U.S. Department of Defense had indeed sprayed South Minneapolis with chemical warfare agents in an effort to make a city become stealth. It was during the time of the Cold War when Russia's military strength was a big threat to America. Apparently the Red Lake Indian Reservation had been sprayed as well. God only knows what the health effects have been on innocent, unsuspecting civilian populations by being exposed to cadmium compounds and other chemicals. I have often wondered if these poisons were the reason for Indian friends telling me, *"Niige, you don't want to mess with them Red Lakers. They fly off the handle too quick, got mean streaks, and even worse tempers."*

I would like to know if the war department is responsible for the permanent addresses of aunties and uncles being group homes and state institutions for the mentally ill. I would also like to know if my government is in any way culpable for the scar in my eyebrow and the medical difficulties my children have experienced. I did get to speak with a woman who had lived in ground zero of the toxic stealth spray. She believes it caused her sons to be born with mysterious medical conditions that were complex, life threatening, and inexplicable. She told me that there was evidence of a generational passing on of ill effects. If America can ever attain the level of democracy we claim to be exporting to Iraq and other places, perhaps there will be hope for my questions to be answered some day.

I'm not going to hold my breath for that to happen. I have to save what breath is left in my tired self to learn about the health effects of something else. I just found out that my children and I were exposed to several years of arsenic, at levels so toxic they were immeasurable, in the soil of the Powderhorn neighborhood home and yard where we lived. The Super Fund came in and removed every milliliter of dirt all the way down to bedrock after the lady who lived there got real sick. She is a gardener. I have a sinking feeling about this and wonder if the arsenic has anything to do with what happened to us. During the years of our descent to different hellacious experiences associated with the onset of my twin sons' various mental health diagnoses, I said things like *"I think we got toxic poisoning from something.*

Maybe it was from using the head lice medications every other month, or from lead paint." Hmmm. You should see what my sons' caseworkers wrote about me in their files!

Hearing the news about arsenic in the yard was like taking a hard sucker punch in the gut. None of the other properties on the block tested toxic—just ours. Hmmm. The news is still settling in and unearths almost too much to consider just now. *Do I contact the boys' doctors? If this is the cause for our medical issues, is it too late to get better? So much damage has been done to my sons' bodies, minds, and spirits at this point, I don't know if it will make any difference to find information. Where would I start?* I couldn't find it on the EPA website. I must admit to having a bad case of the chronic sorrows, complete with an endlessly flowing water feature. Then there's this upwelling of thoughts and feelings that does feel volcanic—its smoky plume the question, *"Of all the eighteen or so houses we lived in, why did the arsenic have to be at this one?"*

This house is the closest thing to *home* my family ever experienced. It is the place we lived the longest of all the houses we moved to, and . . . we lived there twice. Years of happiness spent there were some of the last times when hopes and dreams for our future dwelt in the fullness of possibilities. It was the *home* where my sons and I were a family, where what ripped us apart elsewhere would never have dared to trespass. It was the last place we had lived together in a good way.

The kids and I quite literally lived out in that yard every spring, summer, fall, and winter. My rocking lawn chair was a four-season wonder that held together through several years of yard sittin'. We always had a swimming pool and slippity-slides in the mushy water-logged grass of our summers. My idea for a great toy was a big pile of dirt and mounds of mud for rain shower playing. I learned to grow gardens in that yard. The old men on the block shared their flower seeds and taught me how to prepare the soil for planting the marigolds and cosmos that eventually graced the entire perimeter of our three-bedroom stucco house. Every spring another section of our much-beloved yard would be dug up for placing a cement walkway or putting up the arbor for morning glories to climb. Crocus and daffodil bulbs needed space to nestle through the winter months, so autumn had me digging their circular designs around a stately concrete birdbath. The herb garden was out back, adjacent to where I ripped out the grass for raspberry bush plantings. The boys helped me knock the clods of green sod against a wire fence to loosen compacted dirt into piles, which were then returned to the ground to receive new life.

Am I going to regret instructing my children about God the Creator by teaching them to plant flowers and tend their growth in that yard? How could the place where I learned to experience real joy betray us in such a cruel manner? I gathered enough nerve to drive past 3224 18th Avenue last week. Gone were all the living things my children's hands had planted—that spoke beauty and hope in yellows and orange. There was no sight of the blue, pink, red, violet, and whites that told the story of *Once upon a time we were a family*.

History, Survival, and the Underground Economy

I WORKED FOR A TIME IN A LUXURIOUS GROUP HOME near the eastern suburbs of the Twin Cities, assisting elders experiencing cognitive and memory difficulties. Ten blessed beings were spending their twilight years in as much care and comfort as their money (or their children's) could buy. The home's private pay monthly rent was astronomical, and thoughts of being intimidated by a social atmosphere of concentrated wealth did cross my mind. I needn't have worried about feeling uncomfortable there. I loved that job, and it tops my list of alltime favorite work experiences. The residents may not have known their own names from day to day, but our living room discussion circles around the fireplace rang with perfect recitations of poetry and song from long ago school years. How I enjoyed hearing "The Daffodils" and "I think that I may never see a poem as lovely as a Tree," in tones and meter of ninety-something-year-old voice.

The only social problem ever to concern me at the group home occurred during a family day Sunday dinner, where residents and relations gathered for a fancy four-course meal. The lovely dining room contained two long tables that seated about twenty people that day. My spot at the table was with those who had no company, or whose arms might forget to lift fork, spoon, and drinking glass. The gourmet offerings were prepared and served by a man who dressed in chef whites, complete with signature culinary headwear. He was new on the job and the only person of color in the house.

The comment that our new chef was a colored man who must have quit his other job as a drug dealer to get this honest work sparked an uncomfortable buzz of one-syllable responses—umm . . . ohh . . . hmm . . . yeaaa . . . uhh. . . . Judgment and ignorance were uninvited guests, and I, for one, would not feed them! The hurtful words felt like a bee sting to my ears and my heart. Our party spoilers were quickly shown to the door when I decided to initiate a conversation worthy of the occasion.

Does anyone remember what it was like to live during the years of the Great Depression? was the first thing to pop into my mind. The stock market collapse had ushered in a decade or so of grinding hardship and poverty for millions of Americans, which occurred in a time their memories could access. I figured on hearing colorful and interesting stories about orphan trains, rail-riding hobos, and bread lines that wrapped around city blocks. I wanted to know what they had witnessed as their neighbors and townspeople adapted to such hard living. The answers to my question came as a surprise and a teaching . . . on judgments, surviving in lack, and the underground economy.

Betty was the first to tell about her mother making bloomers out of flour sacks, which opened the door for others to chime in on how scratchy to the skin their underwear had been. Margaret told us how her father's job at the copper mine did not provide wages enough to sustain all eight of his children. Her mother started a home business to supplement the family income by learning to operate a still out on their back porch. The regular chore list for her older siblings included helping to fill pickle jars with home brew and to repaste any falling off labels. During prohibition years, the making and distribution of alcohol was illegal, which called for creativity in business practices. The local haircutter would load wood slat *pickle-filled* crates onto the back of his truck every week, bringing said cargo into town to sell at his barbershop. Amid hearty laughter, someone else spoke of using ketchup bottles for the white lightning and corn whiskey that had been the spirit specialty in their neck of the woods. Someone else mentioned a woman named Carrie Nation who evangelized on the evils of liquid libations, which kept the conversation percolating right on through our meal. It wasn't long before every resident had shared memories of firsthand experiences with family enterprises in bootlegging booze.

Their stories were not told in shame-shrouded whispers, but in tones that were matter-of-fact, although my eyes heard them say something more. Hints of pride regarding their parents' resourcefulness rested in the cornice of up-folding eyelid creases and in cheek dimples appearing on their smiling faces. It looked to me like self-satisfaction invigorated the Sunday diners, as previously slumped shoulders sat back on top of newly erect backbones. Only one person in the room seemed uncomfortable with recountings that included admissions of participation in criminal activity. She kept trying to change the topic of discussion. She was the daughter of John, whose mother distributed dandelion wine by way of castor oil flasks concealed in her midwife supplies bag.

When we finished our dessert, I busied myself helping to clear dishes and refill coffee cups. Holding back my thoughts and opinions on the dinner discussion much longer was going to be a chore. Thoughts had become words in my mouth, quickly multiplying into sentences that might launch if I breathed too deeply. I'm not good at swallowing verbiage that's on the tip of my tongue. On my second tour with dishes, a choking sensation put too much pressure on the back of my throat, which relieved itself by broadcasting the entire reactive contents of my mind in a volume that carried into the kitchen, where our chef was keeping to himself.

Over the din of clanking plates and bowls, I heard myself saying, *"Isn't it interesting that every person living here can remember mothers, fathers, uncles, or other close relations who involved themselves with selling illegal substances? Well, I guess nothing much has changed. Poor people are still doing the same kinds of survival hustles. The only difference is, now-a-days people are selling weed and crack cocaine. Oh yeah . . . the legal consequences have become quite a bit more severe."* I couldn't keep myself from blurting more commentary, even though the nature of what I said could have been the fat lady skating on thin ice while singing the one-hit wonder she's known for—"It's Over." My thoughts and opinions seem to have a mind of their own, as they propel themselves out of my mouth at times when I'd rather they didn't. The doctor calls this impulsivity ADD. The hotwire between my heart, brain, and vocal chords didn't respect the risk of losing my job by verbally offending well-paying family members. The next thing out of my mouth was a depth charge. *"Isn't it interesting that everyone here has a family history of selling an illegal drug called alcohol? And isn't it totally amazing that not even one of you is, or ever has been, a colored person?"* Everybody agreed about that being amazing, and the chef cracked a smile resembling the Grand Canyon during a spring rain. A few weeks later my supervisor pulled me into his office. He told me that family members shared comments about the interesting discussions that I provoked with their parents. Then he said that I should keep up the good work.

What's in a Poem? Introduction to "A Glimmer of Heaven"

THE TIME WAS SOME MINUTES AFTER 4:00 A.M. The window looked over horizon view of Lake Superior, unfolding the promise of a new day. My son had been found in an alley during the early hours of the previous evening with a profusely bleeding head injury and a blood alcohol level of .44. Alcohol poisoned at levels inconsistent with life and breath. The stillness of Jacob's deceptive slumber was an incongruent mother memory that had been the loveliness it is to gaze upon a sleeping child. The sight of him at the intensive care unit recalled emotions that were so many dissonant intrusions in current reality and a terrible similarity to another child's sleep. His twin brother, Isaac, only two years previous, lay the same way—hooked up to gadgets of medical invention that beep and buzz. Their speech in high-pitched tones reminded my body to make adrenaline, even though the sight of sleeping child was peaceful. Yes, I can recall the time was after 4:00 A.M. when I lifted pen to write "A Glimmer of Heaven." My eyes gazed into the horizon, painting itself anew over Duluth's shore on Gitchigumi. Colors brilliant orange and pink, the colors of sailor's delight, were accompaniment to little scribbles upon paper. Stupor of disbelief seeped into the port of my reality, into the pores of time and space suspended in slow motions like the ore tanker gliding into dock. Seven months of Jacob's hospitalization after that evening spent more quickly than the minutes before dawn in the morning when this poem was written. Perceptions of gravity's weight became questions to God regarding when the cruel jokes that are my life would stop. This was the holiday of Mother's Day similar to the one two years previous. The twin child sleeping upon death's doorstep on the exact anniversary when his other half slumbered similarly became their brotherhood's completion and nearly the death of me.

The time was around 4:00 A.M. when I no longer wanted to be alive in my body, in the life unfolding before my eyes, in what it meant to be me in these circumstances. I wanted to lay down and die and be gone from the world of pain. *"It's always the darkest before the dawn, Julia."* Mother's voice insinuated itself into the foggy dark of my suicide's contemplation. The time was some moments after 4:00 A.M. when horizon's first glimmer appeared so far away. The melody of Mama's voice and a glimpse of distant light, the conspirators of my desire for sleep, inspired a poem instead.

A Glimmer of Heaven

Mother's Day 2000, after 4:00 A.M.

I can sense a place that glows and shimmers from above.
The people speak kind words up there—they call the language Love.

I can see a light that shines for you and me
In a place that knows no strife, where captive hearts have been set free.

I can smell a fragrance as lovely as a rose.
It must be the breath of God—glory in the wind He blows.

I can hear a song—voices rise in harmony—
The melody so beautiful that wickedness must flee.

I can taste a sweetness—His word upon my lips—
Christ my only hunger, His Spirit fills me with His gifts.

I can touch God's brilliance as I reach out to His hem.
When I fall and grace has lifted me, God heals me once again.

I can feel a joy—unspeakable and great—
The power so invincible it breaks the bonds of hate.

I can hope and dream beyond suffering and shame
For something that is beautiful—Jesus is His name.

My burden, it is heavy, my strength alone so small.
Come, abide in me, O Lord. Help me as I fall.

For *when*, not *if*, I stumble, trial's lessons I have learned.
Baptized by Your fire that refines me as it burns.

I offer You my praises, my struggles, and my pain.
When the enemy comes against me, You raise me up again.

The fruit of tribulation, the cross that I do bear,
Gifts me with compassion, which I now gladly share.

My Father up in heaven, hallowed be Your name.
Your Son You sent to live in me, and I'll never be the same.

I long to see and smell and hear, to taste and touch and feel
A true and lasting peace this day, a perfect love that's real.

I can see a place that glows and shimmers from above.
The people speak kind words up there—they call the language Love.

Father, Son, and Holy Spirit, please hear me as I pray,
And send a bit of heaven down to earth for me today! Amen!

Song for Jacob

I'm so sorry—I never thought it would be this way.
If I could take all your hurts away,
I surely would.

If I were queen of the world:

I'd make enough jobs for everyone to feed their children.
Families would have a home,
Heat and a telephone. . . . Then maybe parents wouldn't get on drugs.

If I were queen of the world:

I'd throw all the guns away—You could go outside and play,
All your friends would be at the park,
And we could go out after dark . . . just like we used to.

I'm so sorry—I never thought things could be this bad.
I know you're feeling sad
And want to cry.

If I were queen of the world:

I'd make those explosions in your head go away all on their own.
Then maybe you wouldn't feel so alone,
And you wouldn't have to take that medicine.

If I were queen of the world:

You'd always have a fishing pole and a dock.
All the kids in our neighborhood would too.
They'd feel safe—and maybe they wouldn't have to join the gangs.

If I were queen of the world:

Not knowing where you wake never would have been.
You'd never have to leave a place without saying goodbye,
And none of our friends would die . . . before growing old.

I'm so sorry—I never thought it would be this way.
If I could take all your hurts away,
I surely would.

If, When, and Did You Know?

"The rich will need a permission slip from the poor to get into heaven."
—*A Katrina Survivor*

If

- I were Oprah, I'd run for president of the United States, win, and then step down . . . just because I could.
- I were the owner of an inner-city grocery store, I'd allow 10 percent of the carts to be used by people who need them to move.
- I were rich in money, I'd send big fat checks to all the beautiful people in my life who *helped out* during my dark decade . . . and then give a huge check to the Fuller Center for Housing, because affordable home ownership is one of the best poverty-reduction strategies outside of living-wage jobs with medical coverage.
- *Nanny 911* had been on TV when my children were young, I would have seen what a bad idea permissive parenting is.
- I were in charge of education, every school district would have poetry slam teams and English as Performance in their curriculum. Students could letter in poetry just as they already do in sports, cheerleading, and band.
- There were a Pulitzer prize for legal essays, I'd nominate the State of Minnesota ombudsperson for Mental Health and Disabilities, Roberta Opheim, for her "Misuse of the Chips Process" document. (Essay: Are We Failing Our Children and Their Families? Children's Mental Health and The Misuse of the Chips Process. www.wmitchell.edu/lawreview/Volume32/Issue1/9Opheim.pdf)

Coffee and Conversation with Auntie

So, I was on the phone with Auntie Sheila last week, and she told me about listening to a talk news program on the subject of U.S. immigration policy. The social analyst said that if all the illegal immigrants were sent back, the whole mortgage industry in America would collapse. The first thing out of my mouth was that our new neighbors must not have been here long enough to have ruined their credit! Most of the poor people I know, especially if they've come from generational poverty, wouldn't stand a snowball's chance in a blast furnace of qualifying for a mortgage, because of the depths of their debt. Their credit is so ruined it would take three lifetimes to repair—or a winning lottery ticket! Their bad credit is so pervasive that it has leaked into the next generation, from desperate parents who list phones and utilities in their children's names and Social Security numbers.

All That Glitters

Many poor people have been baited by predatory lending practices in the credit card industry and by car title and payday loan companies. I think it is the modern-day version of the company store. Glittering like gold, offers for quick and easy credit arrived in our mailboxes as regularly as rain in the spring. I saw people, myself included, get high-interest lines of credit for use in daily survival—to pay for our children's school clothes, to supplement the monthly food budget, and to stave off gas and electric disconnections—hardly luxury items. We unwittingly harnessed ourselves to a ball and chain that secured our fate to remain in the class of our origin, or worse. For those of us who had attempted the climb up and out of America's underbelly, easy loans became the one straw too many in the delicate balance of our ecosystems. The fine-print consequences for your first late payment—a quickly shifting weight—and author of the cruel joke that is slippery slopes, whose clever punch line is that the safety net for breaking this free fall . . . is shame and self-blame.

A Few Government Programs We Should Fund Fully and Tweak!
- Community Action Agencies
- Upward Bound-TRIO
- IDEA Asset Building Accounts—Create a new category, *debt reduction,* for which this two-year matching savings account could be used, in addition to the current categories of education, home ownership, and starting a small business.
- Heating Fuel Assistance—Fund fully and add automobile fuel vouchers so people can afford to get to their jobs.

- Head Start—Fund fully for all children who qualify and expand to five days a week, extending programs from half-days to at least eight hours to accommodate working schedules of parents.
- Circles of Support—Expand and further develop the model of intentional relationship building across social divides of class. Make sure the staff is healthy!
- Section 8 Housing Vouchers—Current waiting lists in most cities across the United States are several years long, and opportunities to submit applications for that "wait" have been reduced to *one* day a year, unless you're a Katrina survivor. (Way to pit the poor against the poor once again!)
- Allow flexibility of using Section 8 rental subsidies to build equity when possible and appropriate.
- Set rent limits to reflect the true market rates so that people can actually find a rental unit that is within allowable prices before the two-month search limit expires and they lose the voucher they waited years to get.

Consider This

This past year I have watched several popular daytime talk shows explore the topic of debt and how pervasive it is in America today. People who lived beyond their means were invited to share their stories in thoughtful, honest discussions. It was obvious that the shows' producers and hosts had taken time to research the issues associated with money, class, and credit. Apparently the middle- and upper-middle classes of the United States are losing ground in numbers greater than I had imagined. Many people are becoming overextended in credit from trying to keep up with the Joneses and with their appearances. I noticed a generous measure of sympathy for parents who wanted to give their children everything and tolerance for the misguided spending habits of people who are losing their grasp on the American dream of accumulating more wealth than their parents had. We can all understand and forgive people who find comfort from the terror of downward mobility by making sure that their children maintain designer-name school wardrobes and the extracurricular activities to which they have become accustomed. We can't blame them for wanting that new car or SUV in the driveway every couple of years. Hard-working Americans deserve their family vacations, lake cabins, and recreational toys. Put them on a debt-diet that is possible to manage, and don't even think of eliminating their homestead tax credit.

Juxtapose with this—The anatomy of a person's undoing—in part

A single parent becomes delinquent on credit card payments (which are at exorbitantly higher interest rates than her middle-class counterpart), and the collection agency, without notice, takes every penny in her checking account on the first of the month. This action causes all the checks she has written for bills to be NSF, incurring a $29 fee every time one bounces, which is repeatedly. I'm not talking one or two times, but five, six, and seven times through! This NSF fee racket makes it extremely difficult for her to clean up the checking account and repay all the places to which she has written checks, which incur still more fees and charges. She begs, borrows, and maxes out the last remaining line of credit to rescue her banking privileges and her twenty-five-year history of paying utilities on time. Through sheer tenacity and allowing her pride to take a bruising, she pulls it off and satisfies the bank and utilities! By that time she finds out it was illegal for the collection agency to empty the checking account of its contents in the first place. Social Security disability income is in theory (and by law) judgment-proof and, therefore, untouchable. Filing all the necessary documentation in a very specific and legal time frame—proving her source of income to various entities—she tried to recover the modest disability payment from the collection agency and prevent them from taking all her money again. Doing all of this took a lot of time and energy. Good job!

Then the same thing happened again on the first of the next month, and again the next! Despite all the frantically filed paperwork and doing what was supposed to be done to make them stop taking her automatically deposited disability payments, that train kept running. It took her to the neighborhood of the *unbanked*, where check-cashing fees are ridiculous.

She lost weight from stress and eating very little even when she could muster up an appetite. Rumors were going 'round that she was on crack. It was the first and only time she ever considered doing something like selling drugs, which she *did not*, settling for trying to make one good score big enough to stop her slippery slide . . . at the casino. These circumstances were part of what broke her down and beat her into submission with an abusive partner—desperation. Legislation was introduced that year to eliminate the tax rebate for renters.

Did You Know?

- Colin Powell said that the biggest threat to national security is . . . poverty.
- Countless thousands of parents in the United States are told they have to give up custody of their children and do so in hopes of obtaining medical care for their sons and daughters who are afflicted with brain disorders and issues associated with mental illness.
- The United States has more citizens per capita who are caught up in the prison and criminal justice industries than any other country on the planet.
- Kennedy said, "Every society gets the criminals it deserves."
- The single most effective weapon against crime *ever*, was the availability of chemical dependency treatments during the Nixon administration.
- It costs less to house and educate children than to pay for their prison cell when we don't.
- Mother Teresa said she "never saw true poverty until she came to the United States."
- Parents in the state of Minnesota did not have the legal right to *take time off from work* to attend their children's school conferences until 1991.
- Most of the people who knew me first by my "Those People" poem thought I was a black woman?

Why in the world would anyone sign up for those rip-off credit card offers that come in the mail?

She got several credit cards to pay for necessities associated with getting her children back from social services. Child Protection had put them in foster care because they spent too much time being unsupervised. Between the small disability check for two of the children and the three low-paying jobs she worked, monthly income did not stretch far enough to pay for evening and weekend childcare, even if caregivers had been available in the first place. The police removed her five middle-school-aged children from their home on the very same evening she received a Certificate of Self-Sufficiency at the graduating out of welfare—MFIP—Ceremony! Losing the disability payments while the children were in "protective custody," the rent didn't get paid, resulting in eviction orders and the end of her perfect rental history.

Hoop jumping to get her kids back from "protective custody" included completing a myriad of court-ordered parenting classes, family therapy sessions, supervised visits, and budgeting classes, all of which were scheduled around systems, not her work hours. Because two of her children have mental health diagnoses, the family reunification plan hoop jumping was doubled. She got fired from one of her jobs, a blow to future employability, and decided to quit another job to accommodate time requirements for fulfilling the plan. Staying with friends didn't last long because the friends could lose their Section 8 housing subsidy for not reporting she was there, and she ended up in a transitional shelter for women. Under all that stress, on an evening of temporary overwhelm, she went to the bar and got rip-roaring drunk. Despite the fact that she rarely drinks alcohol and has no other substance abuse issue, the shelter staff reported her drinking episode to Child Protection, who then ordered her to complete chemical dependency treatment. Because the shelter requires all residents to participate in support groups in order to stay there, she was forced to give up the remaining job she had managed to keep. And so it goes . . . And so it goes . . .

Company Came Calling

For Cynthia Bernick and Brenda Caya

A cherry when it is blooming, it has no stone.
A chicken when it is peeping, there is no bone.
A ring when it is rolling, it has no end.
A baby when it is sleeping, there's no cry'n.
—Folk Song

Well, look what the wind blew in from hither, thither, and yon!
The articulation of my grief showed up with luggage in amount
Announcing its intentions to stay on for the while that spends leisurely,
Showed up looking for hospitality of conversation and tea, yes,
And didn't even wait to be shown to the guest room.
Dropped its bags in the doorway, unpacking anguish, heartaches, and woe.
The expression of my grief wants to write the book of sorrows,
But will have to settle for this page, and perhaps a few moments of
    sympathy.

Irish washerwoman hands had ever so carefully tucked
And stuffed grief's voice into matching set that hung
Over the shoulder heavy, and zipped into unseen compartments on
    wheels even.
Irish washerwoman hands that hold babies, fold neat creases,
Pressed down her palm the iron's heat.
Her scolding finger magic wand keeping children in line and trouble
    away,
Her hands folding
Grief into prayer could fold a molecule in half if she had to.
Prayers that were cherries with no stone, chickens without bone,
Rings without end, and babies with no cries, got tossed out onto the
    floor by the door.
By the light of my compassion, and by the tune of silvery moon it
    wanted to be.
A melody.
But no.

Thud was sound of grief, echo of solid rock the house was built upon,
Where a dream of home and family once desired to exist.
Met by scorn of neighbors when sod was not the pretty picture in
    time, in the look good.
In keepings up with Joneses, addictions to pretense.
We met ugly faces picketing the weeds in the front yard upon our return
From the funeral of my son's father. The objects of scorn we were.
Our poverty did offend grass police.

Thud was my heart struggling to keep rhythm with disbelief and
    cruel joke
That was my father's passing away, revealing him to have been a
    multimillionaire.
No back child support or recompense for childhood stolen.
We who from his loin did spring were left with umbrellas and such,
While she, already in comfort's lap, who did share no blood,
Inherited the entire sum of his wealth in a trust fund,
Safekeeping 'til reaching the age she is today.
Bone contentious, infection it wants to be.
Washerwoman hands fold trespass into prayer. Lord, deliver me from
    evil thoughts.

Grief cried imperceptibly. Shame silenced unfolding secret from
Being victim of another inheritance. Scam artist saw wound walking
    I was.
The wound fresh, I did not feel pierce of shark hook that kept me on its
Line for three years. Mac daddy played my precious heart and my purse.
Played me all the way out of town, to down and out of my mind.
Debt incurred from my first love affair tipped
The balance of equilibriums,
From shaky stilt walking. All tumbled down.
The sound of crashing glass and twisting timbre.
The sound is falling down into holes. Fraud's deceit sounded loud.
But my grief only whimpered. I actually wanted to wear his ring.

The articulation of my anguish dropped by with intentions
To write lamentations by chapter.
This poem will have to satisfy enunciation's reach for light of day.
Irish washerwoman, her evenings spend earlier than they used to.
Her hands tire easily.
Her tired hands fold the grief that is mother denied,
And child's rightful place with family deprived.
Sorrows with no end deserve their own sad melody.
Irish washerwoman's hand will compose the symphony,
Of babies with no cries, another day.
Her hands will fold the sound of sleeping children into prayer,
While showing her guest to the spare bedroom.

Be anxious for nothing, but in everything by prayer and supplication, with thanksgiving, let your requests be made known to God; and the peace of God, which surpasses all understanding, will guard your hearts and minds through Christ Jesus. —Philippians 4:6-7

Part D. In the Tail Winds with No Construction Materials in Sight

"The Law in its majestic equality forbids the rich as well as the poor to sleep under bridges, to beg in the streets, and to steal bread." (Anitole France)

Born Again?

AFTER MY PERFORMANCE IN A SOUTHERN MINNESOTA TOWN, a woman came up to ask me a question. "Have you been born again?" was her curiosity.

My reply, "Yes, as a matter of fact I have. Several times, and most recently . . . "

On a toe-freezing winter night, a group of hearty college students was gathered around the fire on the plaza of our state capitol. They were participating in a homeless sleep-out. I'd been singing, speaking, and reciting poetry at similar gatherings for about twenty years. This one was exceptional because the young woman who organized it is a social genius! Yes, she is. So I'm freezing my butt off, and who should arrive but Tou Saiko Lee, the word shaman from East St. Paul. He starts spittin' his flow, a piece on living the life of a true poet. Tou Saiko Lee's spitlet dropped on my head. I was baptized into the Holy Spirit. Yes, I was born again when Tou Saiko Lee coughed. He blessed our atmosphere with anointed verses. They danced in the cold air that night of the homeless sleep-out. Ancestors in his breath. Tomorrow and next century on his breath. Power of life in his words, on spit anointed for the occasion of my rebirth. I am thankful for Tou Saiko Lee coughing.

Birds in the BBQ, Chronic Sorrows, and Speaking Life

For Frank Sentwali and Desdimona—Bless you for tending sapling that was Tou Saiko Lee.
  God Bless Melissa Borgman for tending educational reform!

Farther along . . . (goes the song) . . . we'll know more about it. Farther along we'll understand why. Cheer up, my children, walk in the sunlight. We'll understand it all by and by.

My mother-heart hurts. Hot tears (holy water, according to the McDonald nuns). And Hylex bleach washes away rubber skid mark on kitchen floor—Nike or K-Swiss—probably left there from a Monopoly marathon or poker game. My sons Isaac, Jacob, and Daniel's laughter anoints the room and lingers a moment, gives my limbs that do not want to clean or scrub another anything, momentum to clean the back deck. I have to get out there and clean the BBQ—the big, black fancy propane cooker on wheels found down the street with a "Free" sign on it. A few months ago we rolled down the block (my BBQ grill and I), in the company of happy thoughts of sizzling ribs and chicken, corn on the cob, potato salad, family, and anticipation of warm summer celebrations that go on all day and into the night.

I have to clean out the BBQ next, what with the Realtor and couple coming. It wouldn't look good that a bird built a nest on the grill inside. I had left the birds alone, thinking, *Well at least they get to enjoy it. . . . I sure won't.* There they were, nestled among the twigs, leaves, strands of wound hair and straw, and all the pieces of whatever mama could fit into the two holes on its sides. There they were—three dead baby birds being consumed by wriggling maggots. They probably got cooked inside that black hood by the afternoon sun. I closed the lid and moved on to caulking the basement bathtub.

Tempted and tried, we're oft made to wonder, why it should be thus, all the day long. While there are others living among us, never molested, though in the wrong.

The hired help took the last boxes and bags of Robert the free-loading renter to his son's apartment and never came back. They probably got sidetracked by all the pussy and big-booty ladies doing naughty things in his vast collection of pornography that was trying to fall out of the overstuffed containers. I was gonna be lucky to have the house ready to show by 5:00 with all three of us working non-stop. *Move limbs . . . move. Just keep moving.*

Never mind that your mama-heart won't stop hurting and the holy water has never shut off since your shirttail relative (who always had much love for youngsters) told you last week that the youth of today make a good case for retroactive abortion. Eeeeeeuuuuuuuuuuueeeeee. And, oh my, his words felt like a stake through all that is sacred. It was as though time stood still as all my instincts and every cell in my body took notice of recognizing the energy of a dark thing—something very bad that comes from powers and principalities, a curse. And inside, where my spirit-person lives, I was deeply grieved. I spell his words, w-e-a-p-o-n and d-a-n-g-e-r-o-u-s!

Oh, Jules, just forget about that, you need to keep working. Never mind that you paid George from the West End to patch the holes in the walls three months ago, and he didn't show up. Dang, the guys I hired today said they would patch the holes—you can't show a house with holes in the walls. And quit your thinking about the birds, the three dead baby birds. Pay no attention that you have three sons, and what all the Indian friends over the years have told you about birds being messengers. You just have to keep cleaning . . . they're coming at 5:00.

Faithful 'til death, says our loving Master, a few more days to labor and wait. Toils of the road will then seem as nothing, as we sweep by that beautiful gate.

My spirit sister, Jean the beautiful, told me about how we have to repent when we don't speak life into our hopeless situations and difficulties. Now I am wondering if I can repent by proxy for my dear relative who spoke the atrocity he did into the same air that our children have to breathe. The elders have told me about the *power of life and death being in the tongue* and about *speaking those things that are not, as though they are* and that we can *speak things right into existence. In the beginning was the Word,* and the word, after all, does get spoken, and . . . oh my . . . how my mother-heart is broken, these limbs don't want to move, and the taste of salt has been on my lips for so long. Sally Larson, the special education teacher at Duluth Central, says my salty lips are chronic sorrow. Anyway, I wonder if our youngsters are having a hard time surviving in this world and taking their rightful place to thrive and blossoming into the purposes for which they were created, on account of nice adults who think thoughts and speak words against life. I like how Kahlil Gibran says, "Our children are the sons and the daughters of life's longing for itself."

Well, right now I have a longing for adults to quit hating on their coming-up generation. Do you think we could get an "Undoing Hating" workshop going on anywhere? I think I will spend time repenting by proxy for all the nice people who have given up on the Isaacs, Jacobs, Daniels . . . the ones called Sterling, Desmond, Wintersun, my godson Jeffrey, Lydel, Deserai, Tycell, Donna Laquia's son, Johnathon, Jesus, and Claire. Maybe my repentance will help the always-aching place in my chest to feel better in time. Those three little dead birds mean so many things to me just now. Maybe they came to help me in my grieving process of crushed hopes and dreams for my sons, my home, my family, my community, and my BBQ. Those little birds are probably enjoying themselves in bird heaven. I think I will try to listen for their songs and think on this day as part of the cycle of life, death, rebirth, renewal, loss, grief, and comfort . . . that does always come . . . in time. So, in that spirit, I will just decide to believe there are good things coming for me beyond the chronic sorrows and continuously flowing holy waters.

I better get back to cleaning this house. There are many more scuff marks to scrub. The poor Realtor got stuck with me for a client. She had to bring me lightbulbs, garbage bags, and Hylex bleach, and she no doubt thinks I am a nutcase. All I talked about was this Hmong guy Tou Saiko Lee, Teens Rock the Mic, poetry slam teams, and how those kids were speaking out, speaking truth, and speaking life. Oh well, as my sons always say, "It's all good." Hmmm. . . . Now there's a possibility. Yes, Jules, it might really be true that in the end it could "all be good." I think I'll try to feel what it would be like for it to "all be good." Hmmm. . . . That feels a little bit peaceful. Okay, now I'll just say it out loud once: "It's all good." Say it again like you believe it, Julia, "It's all good." God, would you help me to get busy with speaking that truth right into existence? It's all good. It's all good. It's all good. And *farther along I'll know more about it!*

My day of birds in the BBQ, chronic sorrow, and speaking life—getting ready to leave Duluth, June 2005!

Katrina Survivor

I HAVE EXPERIENCED A PECULIAR AND IMMENSE LEVEL of anger this week, brought on by outpourings of generosity and discussion of issues surrounding Hurricane Katrina.

I watched television shows detailing our national response to the calamity. Something in the *body language* of Katrina's victims, the featured guests shown in snippets all week, spoke to my heart and sensibility. Families and other recipients of charity, kindness, and relocation efforts were shown sitting upon carefully arranged studio sets, smiling appropriately. To my eye, they looked like people doing their best to appear grateful. To my eye that is linguistic translator of words unspoken, I wondered if they were thinking and feeling anything similar to what I experienced watching them.

Simmered anger's flashpoint, bits of outrage, and whys?
Surfacing question after question,
Round and round, like the soup boiling,
In the pot, in kettle melting
Pot on the stove. Hot passion of desire for justice.
    Flashpoint. Katrina.
      Questions.

Why is it socially acceptable for Americans to become outraged regarding only certain kinds of human suffering—such as acts of nature that cause widespread homelessness?

Why does it feel as if our generous spirit is appropriate only at Christmas?

We had 3.5 million homeless Americans on any given day before this hurricane, and I didn't see celebrities or anyone else who has too much money being outraged! There are now thirty-seven million Americans living below the poverty level, roughly the whole population of Canada, while we give tax breaks to the rich over and again. People stuck in the permanent underclass of our nation have been living with daily violence, unmet medical needs, substandard education, and, at its worst, Third World conditions for the longest time, all very well documented.

Where has our outrage and generosity been all this time?

I wonder if this was the conversation I heard inside the dissonant muscle tone that was a smile feigned and gratitude displayed for cameras, for us.

Katrina survivor on TV, I heard you!

When God Created You

For Dawn Lyn "Break of Day" Shannon
upon the occasion of celebrating the completion
of a master's degree in Special Education, January 13, 2007

"For you created all things, and by your will they existed and were created."
—Revelation 4:11

When God first dreamed you into existence, dew-laden grass spar-
    kled morning's light. Daybreak is the time of new beginnings and
    transformation.
All your ideas, seeds of possibility, and blessing business
Contain the atmosphere of God's breath, the breeze revolving this
    ball of clay

'Round and 'round the axis of his love for us, for you . . . 'round his Son.

Your nature was fashioned from essence of new day, opportunity, options, and things fresh. That's why your name is Dawn.

When God imagined the purpose for which you were created, his design was precise.

Length and lank, shape and size, he made your hands, and toes, hair, and your eyes. He wished you tall, to have the vision of eagles, the graceful air of queenly authority while walking among the nations, and for when you'd keep company with kings. Your feet have strength enough to teach a generation about standing in the gap for itself, for a future. Your bosom is ample sustenance for education's orphans.

Yes, dear niece, you were imagined and designed with perfection for a day such as this!

When God painted the picture of who your earthly caretakers would be, you were blessed.

His pallet and brush strokes are a masterpiece.

The brown hue of you is warm and rich.

Skin tone is your spiritual inheritance from ancestors kissed by sun-light eternal, whose darkness is the quantum physics that absorbs, retains and refracts full-spectrum Christ light. Your landscape is of your great-grandma's grandma, and the idea of Amenetta, colored by shades of the mathematical equation where: People minus love,

divided by greed and brutality,

plus suffering and struggle,

multiplied by centuries,

equals the sum of

Radical Compassion. You are made from the stuff of miracles and wonders!

God's dreaming of you was probably the loveliest experience of his day.

When God imagined your purpose, he did the world a big favor.

When God's hand drew you, beauty increased on the planet.

Mother Maya was talking 'bout you, girl, just below the angels and all.

Today I give thanks to God for how and why and who he made you
   to be.
He did fine work. Crafting you proves the promise:
That we are created in his image!

Love,
Auntie Julia

The Main Course

I ain't no appetizer you can nibble here and there.
I'm not a side dish either, believe me if you care.
I'm sweeter than dessert and more delicious than a treat.
My fuzzy-navel nectar gonna knock you off your feet.
I ain't a bag of chips you can munch on now and then.
And that's real good for you, 'cuz salty oil is not your friend.
I'm not a Mountain Dew, or a Kool-Aid, or some tea.
A drink of me refreshes and brings serenity.
I'm not sloppy seconds upon a dirty plate.
My portion is enough your hunger to abate.
If you haven't figured out by now, I ain't no
Midnight munchie,
Or the crunchy in the nut mix,
Or the funky fast-food lunchy.
I'm the main course, daddy, Number 1, and one and only,
A feast of finest splendor that would never
Leave you lonely.
I'm the main course, daddy, my plate is all you need.
My taste is that of succulence, nowhere else
You'll want to feed.
I'm not leftover hot dish warmed up in a pan.
My meat is fresh and sizzlin' hot, and kept up for a man.
A man who can appreciate dining at its best,
Saving up his appetite for rib, and thigh, and breast.
You see . . . I'm the main course, daddy, and that's
All I'll ever be. Go ahead and eat your junk food,
'Cuz you won't be tastin' me!

Me and the Lutherans

"Love is our true destiny. We do not find the meaning of life by ourselves alone—we find it with another."—Thomas Merton

SAY WHAT? THE LUTHERANS WANT TO END POVERTY in Minnesota? Wait a minute. I have to get my mind wrapped around this one and check my ears; 'cuz there's something different about these words. The tone in which you speak them is . . . well . . . a tone I haven't heard much outside of the neighborhood. It is strangely familiar, though, like when your long-lost cousins come to a family gathering and you hear strains of great-uncle and gone-home grandma in their voice—familiar like that. I *did* hear you say you want to end poverty in our state. Your words resonate with an energy that makes me feel that you're really serious, piques my human/social/spiritual justice antenna, and sounds like music, even though it's just talk. I let the vibration of your conversation into my sacred space—where hope and faith live—and where your voice and mine can create harmony. Harmonious resonance is a language I understand well. It is a vessel worthy to contain the promises our Creator gives us. So when you come along and speak about ending poverty—your voice ringing with the sound of your faith walk—well, to tell you the truth, those lyrics can make my spirit full with possibilities of all things working together for good! My heart bursts out with verses of . . . you're here . . . you're here . . . so am I. . . . Let's reclaim one another and live happily ever after!

Now that's a big rush of energy! It's very powerful, causes me to be lifted up, and feels sooo good—better than feeling good with booze, or weed, or a first-love high. It's better than chocolate chip ice cream and all the other things that my flesh enjoys and desires to experience. You watching my back like this is wonderful, right up there with fresh baby and answered prayer. In fact, entertaining the possibility of human beings reconciling with one another on the socioeconomic tip creates a chemical reaction of such satisfaction that it should be the singular antidepressant prescribed to treat symptoms of generational poverty! It could be patented under the name spelled H-O-P-E, because that's the transformative power inherent . . . and inspired . . . when you and I decide to work together to end suffering under lack and need. This reconciliation is a pretty big deal. So, to my way of thinking, it is an endeavor sacred that should not be entered into lightly.

Pill popping of the hopeful kind needs to come with a warning label that reads: "Side effects may vary according to socioeconomic condition of patient. For those experiencing poverty: Watch for feelings of fear and anger from past disappointment and present-day struggles. Discontinue use if extreme terror or suicidal or homicidal thoughts appear. After a good cry and loud cursing, begin again, increasing dosage slowly to dissipate leftover hurts from wounds unhealed, until desired effect of well-being is attained." You see, when I open my holy of holies to you—where hope for change *still* lives—it can be a scary experience. I wonder if it frightens you as well. My hope . . . well . . . she's tired, worn, and a bit emaciated. She's been bruised and had both eyes blackened by the world. My hope's been hiding and protective since the last time we were together. She's also been busy, had two daughters to raise. St. Augustine calls them by the names of Anger and Courage. Hmmm . . . I suppose it might be all right to open up just a crack. I am a bit wiser this time around. I'll just be more careful not to let you in too far in—'cuz the last time I did that, you kicked me to the curb when compassion fatigue set in. At least that's what it looked like to me. But how would I know? You went home to the suburb and never came back, didn't say why you left, and never even left a Dear Julia letter. There's so much ground under these feet marked by abandonment that I'm not sure I could trust you if I ever really needed to. But, I will try again. Maybe I can just hang around the Lutherans and put a few harmony notes into the conversation every now and again.

What's that you say? You want to end poverty in Minnesota? And you've set a date? Are you kidding me? That sounds crazy! Wait a minute. I'm still letting the ending poverty part sink in. You say you've created a fifteen-year plan, and it's called the 2020 Vision—A Minnesota without Poverty—Where All Children Thrive. All children? Okay, now you've got my attention. You're not just talking about creating more social Band-Aids for the gaping wound that is America's permanent underclass.

My thoughts go into conversation with the heavenlies immediately. God, could it be true that comfortable people have noticed we are hemorrhaging over here in "Other America"? Could it be that folks are figuring out that social divides are deep cuts in the human body that create and reinforce this "Other America"? Are we realizing that allowing an "Other America" to exist is suicide? After all, you can't live without a heart, and if the poor aren't the heart of God on earth, then I don't know what is. It could be a big reason why God's Son spent so much time and energy instructing on how to regard the homeless, hungry, naked, and imprisoned among us.

Correct me if I am wrong, but wasn't the topic of love and the poor one of Jesus's favorite conversations? His emphasis speaks to me about the poor being beyond precious in the value system of God. Jesus's word directs us toward that which is vital and life giving and could be the key to liberate all of humanity from our selfish selves! I wonder if somewhere deep inside visible and invisible gated communities—purchased by power, privilege, and too much wealth—people are getting lonesome for their heart? Father God, are you giving more people their spirit eyes? Can they see that our life-blood is flowing into prison industry, poverty industry, war industry, diminished lives, and early death? Do they actually care? They're not just talking "cauterize the wound," Lord. The Lutherans want to go after the blade—no, the chain saw—that's ripping the flesh and bone of a people. Father God, I think we need a divine surgeon with a quickness, because your precious ones are getting weak and a little crazy, desperate and unbecoming of all the good things we the poor have always been about. This bloodletting and centuries of our collective degradation are making us a bit soul sick too. Father, I do admit to feeling discouraged and worried about the toll this fever is taking among poor peoples.

In the short speck of time I've been alive, if my vision is correct, I have seen "good things" that have kept the suffering-underneath people near to life and away from soul death begin to melt away like the polar ice caps . . . yea . . . melting . . . and in the same exponentially multiplying manner! Our elegant language of kindness, care, and community is breaking apart—floating off. Our culture of generosity, of sharing our last everything with one another, is sinking beneath the scope of what my eyes can see, and that makes me nervous. People, family, and community have always been the 401(k) and social security plan of the poor. Our relationships have long been the wooden cane we lean on. How can the poor survive without one another? Who are we gonna turn to when the bird flu hits? Father God, *please* help the Lutherans who are gathering to end poverty in Minnesota. Help them to rescue the vestiges of how to *be* with one another, the being together in good ways that some of us grandmas, grandpas, elders, and young ones still know about.

The Lutherans have a fifteen-year ending poverty plan. They sure do like to put time frames on things. They have timed agendas for the meetings, for what is to happen every five to ten minutes. At first I thought it was a joke, but I learned that they are dead serious about timing everything and would probably try to time farting if they could. My friends up on the reservation looked at one of the Lutheran-style timed meeting agendas and wanted me to ask the bishop if he knew exactly how many minutes it will take after we die to go to heaven or hell. I have noticed that Lutherans have lots of meetings to plan more meetings, then they have a premeeting right before the meeting and a postmeeting afterward. We do the after-meeting thing in my neighborhood too. It's called let's go have a beer and Juicy Lucy at Matt's bar! My brain gets very tired trying to operate within time constructs like that, so I have decided to sing at the meetings. After trying to hold a Joy to the World ending poverty singers choir practice that nobody attended, I have begun to bring choir practice to the meetings.

All in all, I have a good feeling about the fifteen-year plan—the incremental vision and timed unfolding of organized intent to end human suffering in our state. Now, where have I heard language like fifteen-year plans before? Oh yeah, in Washington, D.C., a few years ago I heard a man from the United Nations talk like that. It was at the National Coalition for the Homeless Conference. He told us there have been countries in our recent history that decided to end homelessness completely. They had ten- and fifteen-year plans, and the goals were actually accomplished. They wiped out homelessness.

Boy was I shocked to find out which of these countries did so—*they were among the poorest nations on the planet*. Big fat hmmmmmmm. Now I am wondering if there were any Lutherans in their midst and if they figured out how to work together across their social divides, and if we could learn from them. I have noticed how Lutherans stay on a thing. They are dependable and committed, and their still waters run deep. My new friend Murial Simmons, a black grandma from the East Coast who is also newly acquainted with things and people Lutheran, calls them the quiet storm.

So you told me you want to end poverty in Minnesota. Then I told you that this effort isn't a social project for me, that it most probably won't happen on a timed agenda, and that ending poverty work has life-and-death consequences for many of my loved ones in family and community. That didn't scare you away. So, then I asked you how long you'd be around to do this work. You didn't miss a beat, and your answer was a lovely descant I'd been longing to hear. You said, "I'll be doing this work for the rest of my life." My next thought was—I'm so glad you're here. . . . We've been dying to meet you! We've been waiting for you to get here for half of forever. If we could have lifted this yoke of oppression off ourselves, by ourselves, we would have done so a long time ago! I have never been the same since I heard you speak those words. Hope's daughters—Anger and Courage—heard a beautiful melody in your voice. It made them want to come out and put on a harmony. So, what songs can we sing together?

Grace on the Loose!

Been experiencing deep joy these months, such as I have not felt in many years.

It's like I'm under siege by an invasion of the sorrow snatchers.

God, did you put a whole army of Lutherans, young slam poets, and various
   guardian angels on the job of thawing out Julia—heart and soul—from
   deep-freeze?

Grace and resurrection energy is poking and prying in, under,

And through thick skin scabs of surviving hard things.

Grace in my personal space is becoming a more regular occurrence.

I wonder why? I must have missed the part in Catholic catechism about grace
   and just what it is exactly.

This week Nancy Maeker told me it is unconditional love.

She told me that because I asked her, What is grace?

Grace alive showed up and made my spine shiver when Connie Marty and I

Sang together side by side some while back.

Grace comes in my mailbox from St. Cloud.

Baptized by grace spitlets spewed from eternity's belly on a cold night

Tou SaikoWordshaman Lee sprayed me with holy water,
   made tired bones sit up

And say, What? Say Word . . . Say what? Say Grace . . . Somebody say, Amen!

Grace named Annaka & Sharaf moved into my apartment complex.

They cook good vegetarian food and do not hesitate to share it.

Some people, such as Judy Florine, are soaking and drenched in grace.

All they have to do is sit there and breathe grace in and out.

When such people do a thing . . . look out! Listen up!

And pay close attention, for the Creator's unmistakable calling card

Will show up. On it, the words read . . . Perfect Timing!

Breath of grace is elegant through young Maryama / poet / genius / heart-
   truth-warrior. She told me how it was Fred H.'s son who inspired her pen.

Silver-haired grace exponential named Jean and Dede most probably kept me
   from ending it all again and again, through unending hells.

The Weiss family-style shalom and matzo ball grace fits into the life-saving
   category, too—gas & cars fixed on sides of dangerous roadways.

Then there's minister warm from the dryer e-mail grace—zenobia silas carson,

The sho 'nuff walking, talking, writing it ALL down for the sake of grace,
   fountain of grace.

There's Ashley Younique Gilbert grace of hand in the air,
 Palm-up cupping grace running over. And
Grace sliding off tongue and shining through all six-foot something of
Rodney "October" Dixon. He's our 20/20 Vision resident poet,
Marching to Zion with me and the Lutherans and
All the others who are gonna come help us end poverty in Minnesota.
Then grace made home visits. . . . Dr. Mary W. helped me get meds, gave me
    Rilke
 and Connie M. guerrilla prayers and food for Kyalynne & Kylyque, indigo-
    children grands.
Great-Auntie's purple iris gracing Messiah Church grounds, family reunion,
me, and the flowers. Now that's gotta be grace. Thank you Walk with Thy
    Neighbor, Alan Loose, Beth Lewis . . .
Hans, Gennae, Rich, Murial, Tom, and grandmother to many, The Reverend
    Martha Sacred Ground Fasthorse, bringing video ministry to the people.
 Phillips neighborhood homecoming, saying grace, eating fry bread at the
    Wolves Den.
Grace gave me a new song and the desire to hear many voices sing it.
Grace made many singers one voice.
Grace wrote, directed, and performed a gospel song/spoken word version of the
    ending poverty political resolution at some big meetings this year.
(Now there's a new way to bring participatory democracy to life!)
The music is under construction—has rough edges and much potential. To my
    great thrill, it's catching life in our little Joy to the World ending poverty
    singers.
That is definitely the grace of God!
Grace more was singing it over the phone
to dear beloved Pauline Redmond, just before she went home.
Bob Albers, teaching grace at the seminary—Bob Albers, Bob Albers, Amen.
Book-writing angels create grace periods between rent-paying times.
I'll never forget grace-filled Ann Braude Adler's words of encouragement: Julia,
    you are the cork that keeps bobbing to the surface of tumultuous waters.
I'm noticing that grace has a power transformative.
You don't stay the same while in its midst. Grace is alive
when it dwells inside people who sing, share, and care with other people, and
    it multiplies.

Grace is powerful and restorative. . . . I like it very much . . . and
would like to keep more company with it.
I enjoy being in the presence, or near proximity, of grace.
Grace makes me feel good and deeply satisfied.
Blankets of grace from their Poppi's hometown, Guadalajara . . .
cover my sons . . . give warmth and comfort. Joe and Suzie fun-style grace.
* Marge Jamieson, graceful giving, how would I have fed the grandchildren?*
There's been so much new grace on the loose in the realms of me.
I think on why this is so and decide it has something to do with
all of the Lutherans I'm hanging with.
I mentioned this idea to her grace-ness, Saint Paul Area
Synod bishop's associate, Nancy Maeker.
She told me about how grace is a really big deal in Lutheranism.
I'm not a theologian, nor have I spent much time before this year
in Lutheran worship. So how was I to know this?
Grace is gentle . . . came on tippy toes . . . and caught me by surprise.
It's kind of stealthy and quiet . . . like the service I attended at Bob Benke's
*   church.*
Grace, with sprinklings of laughter, forgave my loud AMEN from the back pew
when the sermon stirred my spirit.
Grace does not boldly pronounce itself: I AM GRACE . . . I'M HERE . . .
*   NOTICE ME. Its language is subtle. It inhabits inner sanctum and the*
*   spaces between words of the people and atmosphere where I tarry these*
*   days, like in Nancy Johnson & Shelly Saunders. Now I am wondering if*
*   the slave-ship driver who penned "Amazing Grace" was Lutheran? Pauline*
*   would probably know that answer. And is it true that Martin Luther King*
*   Jr. was named after a certain grace-monger who ushered Lutheranism*
*   into being? All these grace sightings bring to mind the words "As a person*
*   thinketh . . . so they are." Believe I'll get busy . . . . and thinketh and liveth*
*   more on the grace tip!*
By the way, did I mention that my ancestors founded a town . . . named
*   Graceville?*

We the People

Singing Precinct Caucus Resolution, Ending Poverty in Minnesota

We the people of this state,
From different walks and many faiths,
One heart—one voice—resolve to create
A land that will not tolerate
Homeless people, prison industry,
Hunger, and manmade misery,
Children dodging bullets on our streets,
Fearful where to place their feet.

We the people of this state,
One heart—one will—wish to create
A land where children's lives are free
From lack, need, and poverty.
Whereas every child wants to live and grow
In body, mind, spirit, and soul—
It's their God-born right, this we know.
Be us resolved to make it so.

Whereas children all need families,
And young ones do have basic needs,
Like love and care in community
Be us resolved, be us agreed.
Whereas moms and dads and teachers strive
To do our best so children thrive;
Our best has failed for many young lives.
Be us resolved to turn the tide.

Whereas food, homes, and health care should
Be a part of every neighborhood.
That our Creator's intent be understood,
Be us resolved for the common good.
Someone asked, can we end poverty?
If not *we* than *who* said he.

If not you and you and you and me,
Then who'll safeguard human dignity?

We the people of this state,
One voice—one prayer—wish to create
A land where captive lives are free
From hurt and lack and poverty.
We the people of this state,
One heart—one will—from many faiths,
Will sing and dance and celebrate
The day when need is no one's fate.

Meg's Robin

My little children, let us not love in word or in tongue, but in deed and truth.
And by this we know that we are of the truth, and shall assure our hearts
before Him."—1 John 3:18-19

I MET HER ON THE FIRST DAY OF A JOB WORKING with seniors whose
minds, memory, and medical conditions had conspired to make them
heedless of their own safety. Ten men and women lived together in
a rural setting, under one roof of a large and very beautiful home. I
was to work eight-hour shifts providing their direct care. Meg's dark
brown eyes caught my attention. Their twinkle was the nature of mis-
chievous child. They sparkled with light that was visible from across
the room. She introduced me to her constant companion, which
was a catheter bag, and used creative names to describe the anatomy
between her legs, more commonly referred to as *private parts*. Everyone in the bookshelf-lined study laughed out loud, including me
(something I hadn't done in a long time). Her sense of humor was as
colorful and quirky as her language. That room was Meg territory in
the communal home stretching along a piece of northern Minnesota
lakeshore. She had a favorite overstuffed chair in front of a large picture window where mail and magazine reading occupied her attention. Among the considerable number of her print subscriptions were
the *New York Times* and the *National Enquirer*—a reflection of realms

in Meg Olson that were as vast as the span of her ninety-six years. In addition to perusing the pages of her media collection, she spent many an hour gazing over her shoulder out the big window.

"You're going to get a crick in your neck, Meg. What are you looking for out there?" my question asked.

Meg's response eased across the room in low tones that sounded as though she were gargling gravel in the back of her throat. "I'm looking for the first robin of the spring. It is the happiest experience of my entire year. Yes, it is. I'm looking for my first robin."

Ho hum, so what if it was spring. I felt like the walking dead. I couldn't have gotten a spring in my step if there had been a fire to run from. I guess I was depressed. Usually the turn of seasons stirs up fresh desire in my hopes and dreams, but life had knocked me around so much that my affect became flat. Besides, that terrible holiday was approaching—Mother's Day. Every time I'd walk into the study the scene was the same—Meg's neck craning to catch a glimpse of the first robin.

"Have you seen your robin, Meg?" I asked, with barely enough inspiration to make my question even sound like a question.

Oh, the sad eyes looking in my direction did catch inside and pricked at the place where my compassion had once flowed like a faucet, as she said. "It is the thing I look forward to every year, looking for the first robin. But, I have not seen my robin yet. Where are they? Aren't they going to come this year?"

Well, this is a memory care home. Perhaps she has already forgotten seeing her beloved robin. They're out there. I've seen them. Hmmmm. Going about my daily business, the thought of Meg's sad eyes kept dropping in at the doorstep where I used to care about others. Not anymore, though. No, not me. Care? Huh? Who cares about me? No one, that's who. I was getting hardened-heart syndrome. The world gave it to me. But Meg's childlike desire for the simple joy of seeing her first robin stayed with me after work and into the next day.

Then, unexpectedly and right out of the overcast sky of my terrible mood, the thought of finding a little ceramic robin to give to Meg dropped into the realm of my consideration. I treated the idea as though it had been bird droppings that fell instead of the opportunity for my springtime to arrive. Drip. There it was again.

Drop. And again. Drip. Drop. Just like spring in Minnesota, when water runs just about everywhere, the little insistent pitter-patter, was thoughts of an old woman and the joy of her year that is to see her first robin.

I finally went to the craft store. While I didn't find a ceramic robin, I did find supplies to make lifelike nests and found a little red-breasted bird fashioned from feathers. I found an assortment of speckled eggs. I must admit that I had a pleasurable hour assembling this creation. Gluing the eggs had to be just right, and so did making the nest look like a family, with Mama perched over her brood. When robin's nest was finished, I could hardly wait to go back to work and surprise Meg.

The next day I arrived for my shift a bit early to spend an extra minute or two with my new friend. I'll never forget the sight of her kissing the robin right on its beak, saying, no asking, "You did this for me?" She repeated that inquiry about four or five times and kept kissing the robin and marveling at the little bird's nest. Her eyes welled with water that went drip, drop down in sprinkles. She laughed and said, "Look, my first robin of the year complete with May showers!" That was Meg all right, as comfortable in her own skin as anyone I've ever known.

She ended up carrying that little nest with her everywhere, and if she couldn't carry it, the aide did. Nest sat next to her during meals, on the end table in the study, and on the nightstand next to her bed. Over and again she told me, "When I die, I want my robin to be buried with me, right here on my heart. I love my robin, and I love you for making this." I could hardly believe how one little act of kindness could bring so much joy to another person. I could hardly believe it was me who did it. And I still marvel in the memory of how making a bird's nest ended up opening the door for my compassion's return, and for much-needed healing.

You see, I went back to the craft store and got supplies for making lots of nests. I had decided to attach them to a wall hanging of a poem I'd written on homelessness. The big children's mental health conference was coming up, and I made specific bird families to honor many of the men and women in the group of people who had hard lives like mine. We are the Minnesota Parent Leadership Network, a first of its kind in the nation, thanks to Amy Ortega, Brenda Caya, Sharon Mitchell, and many others. I made about a hundred little nests, and my grandchildren even got in on the act. They enjoyed our time together in crafting each family. I can't begin to describe how healing it was to assemble their personalities. Little doves for the nests going to families who'd lost children to suicide or murder. I'd find out if people's favorite birds were blue jays, cardinals, and so forth.

Many of the gift nests had experienced May showers like Meg's robin did. Springtime broke anew in my soul during the time when I first met a gravelly voiced ninety-seven-year-old woman who talked like a sailor and looked at me one day with sad eyes. Creating every little bird family was medicine for healing my broken heart, smoothed the calloused scars left where my own family had been ripped away and ripped apart. The spring showers of my rebirth anointed birds' nests many as they were being designed . . . yes . . . brought much healing . . . yes.

Isn't it amazing? One little act of kindness, the creak of a rusty faucet spigot, became momentum to usher in so many blessings; they rushed as rivers rush in months of thaw. Isn't it amazing?

Here's another something amazing. It was a year and some months later, after I had moved back to the Twin Cities. I was at the state fair with my grandchildren, and tens of thousands of other people, when who did I bump into? I'm not kidding. There must have been between eighty and a hundred thousand people there that day, and I ended up sitting down right next to Dianne, Meg's personal care attendant, who just happened to be down from Duluth for the day. She told me Meg had passed away. She'd been gone about a month. She also told me that Meg's final request was honored. Meg and her little robin's nest rest together in peaceful slumber.

Isn't that amazing?

Birds Live in Nests

Birds live in nests—there's a home for squirrels and bees.
All of creation gets to live somewhere—would someone tell me please.
Why are people homeless? Why are children on the streets?
Why do some have way too much, while others do not eat?
Birds live in nests—there's a home for squirrels and bees.
Mankind has homelessness and people we don't feed.

I'm a mother and a grandma—I've worked hard all my life
To try and raise my children amid heartache and strife
Of being unwanted, the object of scorn,
In part because of a disease my children had when they were born.
They call it mental illness—something 'bout chemicals in the brain.
They blame it on the mother—name us crazy and insane.
We had to live in shelters, and moved from town to town.
Friends and family turned their backs on us—there was no help to be found.

The social workers told me to get medical care for my sons
I'd have to give up custody, so they could access funds.
Mental health care is expensive—families live with untold pain.
But to give up your child 'cuz he's sick is what's crazy and insane.
I did everything I could to hold my family intact.
We lost our homes and cars, my jobs—all but the clothes upon our back.
The hospitals and doctors and systems got paid well,
While my children and I made our way through homeless hell.

Our streets and our prisons overflow with each new day,
For those with mental illness have no other place to stay.
Humanity has technology, and progress and might,
And countless millions of souls have no shelter in the night.
So as I live my life and struggle, sometimes I ask God when I pray—
How can his eye be on the sparrow while my children suffer in this way?
And the free will he gives us, is it a blessing or a curse?
All of creation gets to live somewhere—You'd think people could do no worse!

Birds live in nests—there's a home for squirrels and bees.
All of creation gets to live somewhere—could someone tell me please,
Why are families homeless? Why are children on the street?
Why do some have way too much, while others do not eat?
Birds live in nests—there's a home for squirrels and bees.
Humanity has homelessness and people we don't feed.
Yes, his eye is on the sparrow—He sees all the poverty and greed.
His beloved Son was homeless once—His eye is on the least of these.

Just Like God?

For beloved Cedric "Cmurf" Harris

THIS PIECE OPENS WITH A MEA CULPA. That's Latin for having to do with making confession.

Please forgive the possible offense of my saying that, well, for the longest time Lutherans have looked kind of scary to me, especially the kind that are also of middle-class and Scandinavian extraction. In fact, members of these people groups have long been relegated to the status of my "Those People." Can we talk on the real? It breaks down like this.

I grew up in a family of working- and nonworking-class, semi-wild, passionate, colorful, Irish Catholic, justice-loving, loud-laughing, hot-tempered, intuitively inclined, song-singing, and occasionally known to dial the tele while drunk . . . assortment of folks. Our intelligence isn't limited to academic or intellectual realms. It's very connected to and expressed by our body's fluid, graceful, and sometimes-rhythmic move-ments. I learned to interpret the world and navigate my place in it, with bold road signs marked by emotion, physical stimuli, and survival issues. The in-your-face, to-the-point, life-slapping-you-upside-your-head way of social relations is the cultural dialect with which I am most fluent and comfortable. My sensory-emotional IQ is quite developed, but I never learned subtle 101.

People who don't visibly emote inspire my fear, because their body language is difficult to decipher, hence there is no way to gauge personal safety. I have rarely heard Lutherans shout "Hallelujah" at church services, nor have I witnessed many comfortable people let loose in public with tears of joy, sorrow, or any other type of moist eyes. I imagine getting snotty-nosed while in the company of . . . humans, fits in this category as well. Controlling one's flow of emotions and responsive bodily fluids is something totally amazing to me. It could be compared to the flesh-taming disciplines of Tibetan monks who fluctuate their body temperature with meditation, or to the physical feats martial artists are known by.

Not to say that mastery of one's emotions is bad, no, not at all. It's just that in all my years of growing up in Minnesota, the polite and more-quiet-than-I'm-used-to people have looked a little like our landscape in the depths of winter—buttocks squeezing stiff, and frozen. Maybe their cold-climate ancestors survived the Ice Age. Their blood could have all rushed up into their heads, stayed there, and left tension in the limbs for the last century or two. That could explain where the physical state of uptight originated. As a matter of fact, this phenomenon has been the topic of socioanthropological commentary down in the neighborhood of *Other Minnesota*. We've been known to say such things as, "You know when the ice people cometh, 'cuz they sound like squeak-squeak when they walk."

All right, yo mama–style, socioeconomic analysis aside—here's the point of this page. It's a lesson on judging people by how they *look*. You see, last fall, 2006, when I fell in with "Those People"— those Lutherans of mostly middle-class, Scandinavian extraction—my essence had been dulled by heartache and hardship many, the temperature of my spiritual countenance plunged frigid, with no home-fires in sight. What did God do? He sent the *frozen-looking people* into the atmosphere of my daily doings. It was then that the unfolding miracle of my resurrection began. The care, community, encouragement, compassion, intelligence, and friendship I experienced ushered warmth enough to plumb the glacial-depth tomb of my soul.

Here's the kicker: Meaningful, authentic connection with this lovely menagerie of folks generated heat that softened a hardened heart and melted the log icicles obscuring my vision. I have a new appreciation for the scripture that tells us, "My people die for lack of vision." As my visual perceptions did their shape-shifting thing, my rigid, inaccurate thought patterns dropped away. It was then I could see who the frozen one really was. And it was *me*! LOL. Who would ever have thought this one up? Not I.

Now, ain't that just like how God does things? Yup. I have noticed how he likes to use the ones we least expect, or have written off, or stand in judgment of, as vessel-blessing bearers that satisfy our hearts' deepest needs and desires.

Now, ain't that just like God?

"If you have come to help me you are wasting your time, but if you have come because your liberation is bound up with mine . . . then let us work together."
—Aboriginal Australian Woman

Psoem in Six Movements:
Rant/Ode to My Desire for Change

Thankful to Bruce Axelrod for turning me on to Poetry
Rodney Dixon, Jamie Wynn, Ashley Gilbert, Kelsey Van Ert
for Spoken Word Poetry

Part 1—The Muse and I

This week the muse came knocking at my door,
dressed in clothes I've never seen him wear before.
He looked so fine.
The tempo of his walk and language
bore a strange familiarity to another guy, the one who caught my eye
when the teens rocked the mic. Last year.
Became the object of a new infatuation.
So muse, strutting his stuff in thuggish-looking duds that were stylin',
beguiled me by making it his business to know just what I like,
spiked our drinks with a pint of potion #9. I can't tell a lie. It's true.
I got a crush on that other guy, and he's younger then me, too. Woo-hoo.
Sipping the beverage got me tipsy and confused, but amused,
as the very next drink made me think I was out on the town
with the guy whose edgy swagger caught my delight.
He goes by the street name slam poetry. Swept the ground from
    beneath me.
We had a blast, the night went by too fast, and we danced ourselves
    delirious, then eloped.
Felt like a dream, but it was not. I was lucid when we jumped the broom.
He crooned, I swooned, we spooned, over the moon,
I blew up with the tune of this love child. It sings.
Slam poetry sweet-talked himself all the way to the altar
    of my possession.
Joy replete was time defied, space between words, shine in rhyme.
Exciting words enticed our conversation to get its groove on.
Made me feel like I was sixteen again, only better than when that was when.
He caressed the sensibility out of my sentence structure,
undressing my expression, in voice suave. Said it mattered not

that my language didn't smatter in the dialect of kings
    or ring academically.
Function of my literacy stood naked in the mirror.
Laid fear of linguistic impropriety in a pile of disguises on the floor,
limp smile upon its sullen heap, humiliation became.
Liberation from confines of heretofores and how to cross the t's
    unequal yoke
with songbird passion-speak. Felt so free. Released.
A chemical reaction, satisfaction it was, and is, and will be.
My seduction was lovely and complete. Muse outdid himself this time.
Charm personified finessed these verses in my ear. I wrote them
    down so you could hear this lyrical attempt. Cedric said that some
    think poetry is depression on the stage.
My intention for this page is desire to inspire and communicate, not
    to frustrate.
So here we go into this flow, this moment in time. We glow. We shine.

Part 2—Freedom Train

People get ready, there's a train a comin'. Don't need no ticket, just climb
aboard.

 I can hardly wait, want to celebrate. Free tickets to a party on a train?
When we gonna break into the wine and drink a toast?
Who will be the first one to sing?
I want more celebration, less consternation. Why we hesitatin'?
Cadence of guns, crack cocaine, and slums
is rhythm diametrically opposed to my nature.
The precisely calibrated electrical impulse that throbs in me and we
    does not,
nor will it ever, jive with poverty's backbeat.
The sound of lack and waste
is orchestra of noise to the cacophony of dissonant syllables.
How do you put a harmony to that?
Who would bother to try? Besides the beast, that is.
And when's the real party gonna start? The one with a heart, a guitar,
    and some soul?

I can almost hear that whistle blowing . . . in the wind . . . whistlin'
 . . . in the wind,
through rustling leaves the trees singing, high-pitch lone melody
 whistle whispers.
Whistle . . . in wind whispers. There's a train a comin'. Change is
 gonna come.
There's a train a comin'. Change is gonna come. There's a train . . .
 change . . . is gonna . . .
Change . . . won't you come by here?
Tone and timbre of unchecked greed hurts my ears, magnifies fears,
 causes tears.
Generosity, won't you come by here, too?
Music of the world's discontent is social plaque,
blocking flow of wealth, and health and energy in my day,
won't let children play. The locomotion's comin', and it's not an
 orphan train.
Symphonies of our free will, written in the key of seven deadly sins,
crescendos of crap lapping up on humanity's shore,
lie-spittle foam cresting on the shoreline of River Jordan,
on the shores of God's heart, for prodigal children we be.
On the shoreline of God's desire for us to live in the abundance of his
 creation.
On the shore of his perfect sacrifice,
where truth and beauty commingled with night,
and birthed my eternity.
Oh, that I may raise a glass to the name victorious, on those shores.
What time, pray tell, will the party be starting?
I'm ready to sing with Mahalia and Marvin,
and Johnny and June, my mama and Martin.
Music . . . won't you come by here?

Part 3—Missin' Papa
I don't care at all for the choir director who fell from the throne.
And who let hell get so much radio play every day?
Did fallen angel flute tune lure fathers away,
To boardrooms and war fields of predator and prey?

It makes common sense that a child's best defense might be a daddy
   at home.
So many left alone for long spells in time, I think it's a sign.
Made a hole in our soul, then turned to a curse, got rehearsed,
   ad nauseam,
through generations . . .
of woman, and boy-child and girls. It's true.
You been missin' Papa. I miss him too. So sad.
How 'bout a family reunion on that train we waitin' for?
Restoration . . . won't you come by here?
The sacred place that got disgraced when earthly fathers went away
became a wound of proportions profound until this very day. We pray.
And we try to soothe the pain,
by joining the religious order of things owning. Can I get an Amen?
We fill our lives with stuff, but it never is enough, and the hole in our soul
becomes an affliction of addiction to a line, or a slot machine.
   Makes me feel sublime,
for a time. Relief does not last, goes away so fast, and the pain is the same
   one that wrote the refrain, "Wasted Away Again in Margaritaville."
Hmmm . . . Not quite the song for the party I'm waiting on!
Neither is, "Where Have All the Fathers Gone?"
We got mamas missin' on the block. Shepherds can't control their flock,
we worship at the temple of the stock . . . market.
Hickory-dickory-dock, workers punch the clock.
CEO's pink-slip portfolio scandalous decree, fornication under con-
   sent of the king.
Or in vernacular of the working poor, it's rape. Plunder the money, I
   don't think it's funny.
Clap our hands to the beat, in the church we built on Wall Street.
Work will make you free, the song that we repeat.
And the feet of our children
keep marching off to war. What for?
For somebody else's bottom line. The *New York Times* is where you'll find
   the scripture of the stock exchange, where the only crimes
that stick . . . do so . . . if you're female. Now where's that case of wine?
This world's become unbearable.

I'm getting hypnotized and hysterical.

Here's the thing . . . I want to sing. What's that sound in the wind?

And when does the party begin?

Tic-toc dickory-dock . . . tic-toc . . . change is a comin' . . . metaphysical train track heartbeat echo backdrop nonstop . . . tic-toc
. . . change is gonna come . . . there's a train a comin'. Change is
gonna come, there's a train a comin' . . . tic-toc, dickory-dock . . .
tic-toc, dickory-dock

Healing . . . won't you come by here?

Part 4—Motherless Child

Hush little baby don't you cry. You know your mama was born to die.

*If livin' were a thing that money could buy, you know the rich would live and
the poor would . . .* We're dying on the vine from poverty systemic,

epidemic that's endemic to the core of belief.

Like a thief in the night we tolerate showing hate

by how we divvy up our budget, and it really is a shame. Cruel game.

But, if we change the name, of poverty . . .

to something akin to bird flu

or hellified soul sickness, list it in the diagnostic manual of ailments . . .

Would funds increase to eradicate unprecedented cause of death and
destruction?

Would it come again no more to blame and scorn

The souls born at the door of poverty and lack?

Might wrongful accusations ended

bring us back to a rational national state of mind?

Has there ever been one?

Convicted by the error of our ways, clarity could adjudicate justice
meted out

by mercy fabricating medicine moralistic, inoculating delusions nihil-
istic, alleviating symptoms of confusion.

Germs of stinking thinking infect imagination with tendencies lower
than the animals,

on the borders of barbaric. Clerics spoke.

Hallmarked by conditions where some get to eat and others don't,
left unchecked.

Illusions of false entitlement, narcissism's trajectory prognosis is
    fatality diagnosed.
Its cure was in the news two thousand yesterdays ago.
A treatable disease it was declared, and we were spared from famine's
    ravage after all. Consideration for the least of these. Lord, please.
Babies raisin' babies . . . all alone . . . it makes me crazy,
got no hope, no home, they're jones . . . .en'
for that next drop of love to trickle down in drips.
Trickle down economy,
tool we choose, innocence abused, confuses sensibilities. Not astute.
Pollutes spiritual atmosphere with lies about scarcity. We believe.
The lie becomes internal, goes against my maternal instincts
on the subject of basic human needs.
 And is it true that what is loosed and birthed here on earth,
is likewise thus in heaven? And, if so,
What will happen to the babies
who suckle on the drizzle-dripping trickle-down seeds we sow?
    I want to know.
Does the dove have an opinion on spiritual economics?
Wisdom, Comforter, Love . . . will you come by here?
Wipe the children's tears, calm the fears, have ears,
to hear the sound of tragedy, profound calamity, catastrophe.
Babies' battlecry. They die. So do we.
Or so my auntie told to me, and she is one to know.
God shows her revelations, situations in God's heart.
Like orphans and widows, and passing through a needle's eye. Why
    try? But we do.
Auntie told me many things, and most of them are true,
some became the wooden cane I lean on lest I fall.
My demise to forestall. She said, "*If it's happening to one, it's happening
    to us all.*"

Arms that should be holding the motherless child
have a new name. Nuclear suicide. We sigh.
Don't tell me that I care too much, or call me codependent.
And yes, it will be other people's lives

flashing past the eyes of my mind when I die. So there.
Take your psychoanalysis and put it in the sun,
then maybe this theory will grow a smarter heart. I'm almost done.
The thought of even one child motherless,
anywhere on earth, still hurts.
And no, I'm not gonna get over it.
Have you ever heard of standing in the gap?
Someone did that, for me, on Calvary.
So I'm giving back, returning the favor.
I hear the glory train comin', clickety-clack . . .
Hope . . . will you come by here?

Part 5—Tedious Journey

Just yesterday morning, they let me know you were gone.
Poverty, the people put an end to you.
Predatory lending, pretending to be your friend.
But in the end, apostles of misfortune get your car, possessions, and
    credit rating.
Debilitating. Facilitating the separation of you and your money.
    No reparations.
Legal loan sharks by name of paycheck and title loan, romance,
refinance, and rearrange your circumstance.
Send you to the poorhouse after taking yours, in foreclosure, disclosure
written in the fine print, you missed about the interest.
Dismissed, blissed by relief from stress, in pending disconnection
of the heat, and pressure from wondering what the kids would eat
    that week. Oh my.
I've been there. At the time not aware.
The fine print really said usury, sucker, makes my mouth pucker to
    voice this admission. Conditions for repayment and of my situation,
    upon contemplation,
reveal I was a victim of fraud.
Yes, I used my legal name, but just the same,
desperation cosigned the contract. Sad fact.
Designed my undoing, felt horrible.
Contractual obligations, stipulations, complications. Author of

impossible situations. Worthless checks, heaps of shame and pain,
goes against my grain.
Privilege of paying hefty fees at the check-cashing stores,
where the ladies are so nice, and I'm not.
Let this little refrain be a warning. Don't entertain anyone by the
name desperation.
Identity thief. Deceiver. Make you believe lies about yourself that are
not true. Boo-hoo.
What's this world comin' to? Let me ask you.

Everybody wants to go to heaven, but nobody wants to die.
Everybody wants to know the reason, without ever asking why.

Jails and prison industry, no guarantee . . . to be free
Unless you can afford a lawyer. What would Tom Sawyer say about that?
The history books told me,
my citizenship a warranty
To life and liberty, could someone please help me see,
Why my sons' brain injuries
get treated in a jail cell, or leave them on the streets?
At least behind bars they get to eat,
and don't freeze to death.
I'm thankful for this little measure of peace,
but every year I cry a tear when I hear the names
of those who died while they were homeless, in Minnesota.
Land of ten thousand social services,
nervousness this causes in the logic of me.
Sometimes all I see is the pimping of the poor by poverty professionals.
Don't get me wrong. Your efforts I appreciate, but
could we negotiate a different solution? Please, Lord.
Where one group of people won't have to make their living
off the backs of the preplanned suffering of others.
I object to the misery by design for the public left out of
public policy.
In Economics 101, I learned free markets won't function at the point
of full employment. This fact annoys me. Disparity we create.

Then ameliorate this discrepancy with safety nets that are not. Destroys human dignity.

Convinced that we're lazy when we can't feed our families. We're defective, inadequate, deficient, and problematic.

Our deficiency, currency valued by poverty industry.

Our value reduced to identity of victim. We learned how to get food stamps.

We learned to exchange our new identity for leftover crumbs from thems that got, and God bless the child that's got his own.

We learned. It's been a slow burn. It hurts. It's hurt several generations now.

We learned hoop jump dance steps admission to Cabrini Green public housing high-rise. Then we learned to survive it,

hellaciously audacious social engineering at its worst. Planned ghetto.

Robert Taylor homes. Thirty thousand strong, stacked up along freeways,

demarcation zones, corridors of delineation between the civilized and orchestrated chaos.

We endured frequent occurrences dramatic and traumatic, exacting emphatically

upon our nature. It was fight or flight stress response, adrenaline elixir it was,

too many situations with consequences life or death, it was too often death it was, survival it was how our bodies got hotwired for addiction.

Our learned behavior may be considered dysfunctional, but its function

got us through travail and hard times. We survived. Now we want to thrive.

We name our birthright. We claim our inheritance. We thrive.

Part 6—Strangest Dream

Last night I had the strangest dream, I ever had before . . .
People in the belly of the beast woke up after sleeping

through a century or two. The hundredth monkey broke through, membrane.

Civilization's conscience birthed
in contractions

of American Dream it was for some who slumbered fitfully,
in contractions
of American Nightmare it was for those who suffered so, but continue to endure.
We beheld beauty. We beheld the promise fulfilled. We beheld the
new creation.
The baby gave us strength,
to wash blood from our hands, the afterbirth was such a mess. We
confessed.
The next order of our business was to plan a great feast. The train came!
It was that party I'd been waiting for. The wine's time was finally right.
Train whistle blew so loud, drew a crowd, we boarded. All 'board.
It was the party of my heart's desire. I sang, you sang, and so did the
saints!
Reconciliation got served in heaping measure, brought pleasure, treasure,
Commensurate, portions of release from bondage was experienced
by all. We bawled.
Then came a course upon plates large in size. Answered prayer realized.
We apologized for slavery in every way shape and form. Terrible storm,
that shook foundations of all humanity's sanity,
nearly ripped our heart from existence. Jim Crow,
strange fruit, nine-tenths a human, deadly lies. Got soaked in balm of
Gilead,
till whole again humans felt. Felt wounds generational melt away.
What a day.
Repent we did. Reparations made. Everyone got paid their forty
acres and a mule,
and all the school one could ever want or need was free.
Serenity pervaded people's neighborhoods. Our mood was good.
The apologies extended. Colonization ended, and then we
caught up on Turtle Islands back rent. Heaven-sent. Unconditional.
Addiction-based economy of gaming ain't traditional,
or healthy in the end. We spent,
money and time giving back what was stolen.
The spirit of manifest destiny got evicted from the rest of me . . . and you.
And we truly felt sorry for promises unkept. We wept. It was holy water.

Someone started singing "I have been released." Troubles ceased.
The feast was lovely, magnificent, and beautiful. As was the singing.
Wine never tasted so fine.
It's vintage was perfection, went with the next course. Dessert it was.
    Debt canceled.
Jubilee cherry, flavor savory in every way. Fruit of the vine and field,
was out-of-this-world delicious and off the chain. God blessed the cook.
Forgiveness
served it was
in unending portions
at the all-you-can-eat buffet
on the dining car of the train
to glory
where the party
among friends
never ends.
Amen.

Just This Week

Just this week, I erased Sharon Keating off the caller ID,
And finally washed her bed clothes—
Another "goodbye, Mama," in the unfolding final farewells
That come, and go, and come again.
They ride the crest of grief
in swells that rise up and spill down my face.
The McDonald nuns call tears holy water.
They spill out till they're done.
They usher in the void where
phone calls many—
bowel stories and requests for Subway, Hardees, and Ho Ho's
    Chinese Chicken Sub-Gum—occupied conversation.
Just this week I thought about how
Mother loved to send ornately religious Christmas cards.
They would have been in the mail by now,
Along with crisp dollar bills for grandchildren & great-grands.
She left just before Jim's, Jane-Anne's, and my birthday—
Fruit of her womb. Hmmmmm . . .
    December 4th was a day with new contemplations
of Mom and me . . . and we.
Just this week,
I remembered how mother told me Auntie Carolinda
Got her the pretty pink sheets and comforter
Dressing the bed where praying the rosary
And communing with EWTN's Father Grochelle
Were an every night ritual.
Sufferings offered up to the heavenlies
Was the continued theme.
Just before soap and water washed away her silver-white hairs
And scent . . . which did linger on the pillowcase,
Her nighttime rosary slipped out 'tween the folds in the fabric
Right into the cup of my hand.
I suppose she's still tryin'
To get me to come back to her beloved Catholic faith!
My granddaughter Kyalynn thought the bedding was so very lovely.

I'm planning to give it to her for Christmas.
This week marked a month and some days
Since Ma got up out of her hospital bed
And went home.
Just this week,
Expecting her to be on the end of every phone call lessened a bit.
Just this week,
Realities of catching up with work and tasks left undone these months
Came crashing through the haze of suspended time and space
That was midwifing Mama into her eternity.
Just this week,
I realized more how precious family ties are . . .
And that I most probably will not be able
To send out Christmas greetings . . . by way of mailbox.
Now I gotta end this poem, 'cuz
The TV she gave me just turned channels again . . .
On its own. . . . It's making loud static noises.
She always did have an effect on electrical appliances, didn't she?
I don't want this week to pass
Without sending much love and appreciation to family and loved ones.
Bless you this Christmas season and always.
Peace,
Sharon's daughter, Julia Dinsmore

Dear Mother

I'M ALMOST DONE WRITING THIS, MY FIRST BOOK OF STORIES. Been pushing past all the mixed-up feelings about my bad spelling and creative use of punctuation symbols. Shelly Saunders, of editorial divinity, is helping me with all that. By now, you're probably floating around with your mother, looking from a heavenly vantage point to see that this is not the *Mommie Dearest* book you feared. I have tried to honor life experiences with truth and authentic recollections. I must admit to feeling relieved, though, that you died before this book was published. I was afraid of accusations, of being the possible cause of a shame-induced heart attack to you or Grandma, as was threatened back in 1992 when "My Name Is Not 'Those People'" was published in the *Minneapolis Star Tribune*.

My talking about *P* word issues always got you riled up. I'm so glad we won't be going there again any time soon—You'd wear me out! In fact, I can still feel the sting from oft-repeated arrows hurled hot off your untamed tongue. I, with my constantly troublesome circumstances, was your most reliable target. You said:

"Julia, why do you insist on living like a shanty Irish? I raised you better than that. We come from proud lace curtain and brick house Irish. You bring shame to the family. Grandma and Aunt Kit McNally might roll over in their Graceville graves if you don't hurry up and change! Just look at your life— Your own brothers and sisters don't even want anything to do with you and all your problems."

I said:

"Ma, they don't seem to want much to do with you either, so who's the pot calling the kettle by disparaging names? Don't you think it's a bit coincidental that we both share similar struggles in this life, such as being welfare mothers and dealing with chemical brain disorders? Do you suppose that their avoidance of US might have something to do with their own unresolved issues?"

Your verbal volley shot back across the room or the telewires with quiver quickness. *"Your life, Julia, is completely unmanageable. I didn't have problems like you do. I never had a bad check in all my life, and the bills were paid on time—after I left your father that is. I always sang my troubles away. What do you do to help yourself? Jesus, Mary, and Joseph, pleeeaase send my daughter to budgeting classes. She can't manage her money, and I just can't stand it! Moving all the time and can't care for your sons properly. Shades of your father you are, cut from the same cloth, reckless and uncaring about how you affect me! Get thyself to an Al-Anon meeting!"*

The pitch in my voice became operatic.

"But, Ma, how can I budget what I don't have? Back when you were on welfare the buying power of a dollar was a gazillion times what it is nowadays! Your rent wasn't exorbitant, the neighborhoods were safe, and you didn't have to worry about your kids getting shot on the bus stop! And, for your information, I am me . . . NOT my father. Geeeze, what is it? My siblings think I'm their mother, and you calling me shades of my father. A person could have an identity crisis in this family!"

Then you said:

"Why do you think WCCO named that _ _ _'n documentary they made on our family ALL ALONE . . . TOGETHER? Buck up! Get over it! Get a real job, get any job.

You're leaning so hard against victimhood, I can hear it squeak! Wa Wa Wa."

Then I got mean:

"And you can't carry a tune anymore, even if it was in a bag!"

You got the final word:

"And if a frog had wings, he wouldn't bump his rump when he jumps! Get over yourself."

Sometimes I didn't bother to argue with you. Sometimes I didn't have the stomach for the pace of flesh-piercing projectiles, much of which sourced from the reservoir of our own pain. On occasion I slammed the phone down hard so you'd hear how pissed I was—especially when a kernel of truth got my blood boiling.

Ma, your quick wit, outrageous humor, and hot temper were unmatchable. Even after all the years of body and brain bathed in high-level doses of psychotropic, passion-dulling medications, I couldn't last much past two rounds of verbal sparring with that mouth of yours. Touché!

In my growing up years, you used to tell me, *"The rich get richer, and the poor get poorer,"* and that *"America is full of gulping consumers,"* and how we should *"stop being such greedy warmongers."* You seemed to have a heart for the underdog and for people caught in certain social unfairness. These topics were the frequent object of your pontifications. I have to be honest here. It hurt really bad that you continuously blamed me for circumstances in my life that were totally out of my control and which I did not create. Your compassion for underpersons did not extend to me as much as I would have liked. I didn't want a pity party. I just longed for the day the blame train would stop its crushing runs over my heart. As smart as you were, you never acknowledged truths in the defensive retorts that were my part of our mud-slinging bouts. The other thing that crushed me was when you threatened to offer up your sufferings for the sake of President Bush and say the rosary for him as well, instead of for me! Grrrrr.

So, now you are gone, Mother. Someone asked me last week how it was going with the loss of you. I told them our boundary issues have cleared up remarkably. I've kept the can of Coke you left at the hospital. It's standing just in front of a collection of your pictures, next to the trio of ceramic singing nuns, complete with a guitar, that used to grace your apartment end table. The candle from Grandma Hilda's funeral stands with the little friar who's playing a flute. This week's addition to your shrine is a pretty painting with the words *"I am taking care of myself today"* perched upon the frayed-edged third printing of your *One Day at a Time in Al-Anon* book. I hope this collection reassures your worrisome mother heart. After all, isn't that all a mother ever wants for her children—that they learn to take care of themselves? I am. My writing corner overlooks the weeping willow and pond beyond glass sliding doors and screened porch. It is positioned so that I may gaze upon the little party you are enjoying upon my kitchen table. Thoughts of you, your mama, and the family reunion that must be taking place in the heavenlies make me feel good. With the nuns' musical accompaniment, I'm quite sure you are singing in beautiful harmony.

When we were coming up with descriptive words for your obituary, Gigi remembered a hospital stay when you kept calling the police. Convinced that the doctors had hooked you up to the Christmas tree to source the power of its blinking lights had you undone with anxiety. I suggested we call you an illuminating personality. Your eyes did always twinkle so.

This week Isaac and Jacob shared memories of how you used to pay them 50 cents to listen to your weekly Bible study at the cockroach house on 22nd. Your dear cousin Kathy wants one of your teapots. I couldn't decide which one to send her, so they're both going to be mailed to Palo Alto.

Speaking of Kathy, she shared a funny little story about you and Dad going on a double date with her and her flame during the year you had five children in diapers. At the interment in the lovely green-walled mausoleum, as your loved ones gathered around the box containing dust and ash of you, Kathy's memory of your night on the town popped into my head and jumped to the tip of my tongue. I'll bet you're proud of my newfound skill with verbal impulse control. I decided that moment might not be the right time to tell about your adventure to a strip club. It was told to me that the evening had been orchestrated to give you a break from poopy diapers and domestic doldrums from long months spent housebound with little ones underfoot. Apparently the evening's entertainment did not meet with your satisfaction. As the four of you were sipping drinks and watching scantily clad women shake their behinds across a stage, speaking your mind from the top of your lungs, these words bellowed through the nightclub. "*Butts and more butts! Butts, butts, butts! I see too many butts at home every day! Looking at more butts is not my idea of fun. Take me somewhere else, and take me away from all these butts, NOW!*"

Yes, I behaved myself, bit my lips, and left this story untold during the somber moments that lingered right before your li'l sis, Carolinda, climbed a ladder and put you into your final resting place. She looked so very brave and tender all at the same time. That moment was full of ancestral ambience. I had the urge, but resisted it, to run out and get the Mexican serape out of my trunk so you'd be wrapped up nice and warm when Auntie put you to bed.

I tried to be a good daughter in your last years and months. I did the best I could to be there for you and, thankfully, have very few regrets. You know by now that you ain't easy to be around for prolonged periods of time. I just said ain't, and your hand didn't reach out from the afterworld to slap my face or accuse me of acting shanty Irish. You're really gone.

Ma, I'm sorry for saying you couldn't carry a tune.

Much love always,
Your Julia

I Call Myself . . .

I call myself . . .
Storyteller, artist, social change maker of twenty-five years,
Working to end poverty and homelessness,
Singer, songwriter, learning to practice Christianity,
Becoming a servant kingdom builder,
Generosity, and beggar in the land of plenty.

I call myself . . .
Daughter, sister, mother, auntie, cousin,
Grandma, lover, friend, ally, mentor, neighbor,
Student, teacher, seeking after justice and mercy,
Claiming the birthright of my spiritual inheritance,
Respected because of who my enemy has been.

I call myself . . .
Wisdom, fool, sinner, redeemed, hospitality,
Abandoned, scorned, judged, unwanted,
Wounded and broken, victorious, restored,
Remade, refined, renewed, remarkable,
And a precious unfolding of creation,

Most important of all,
I call myself . . . Child of God.
When I can know myself as such
A promise is born.
It is by answering to this name that
I can call you . . . Child of God too!